40 Days

Toward a Servant Leader Mindset

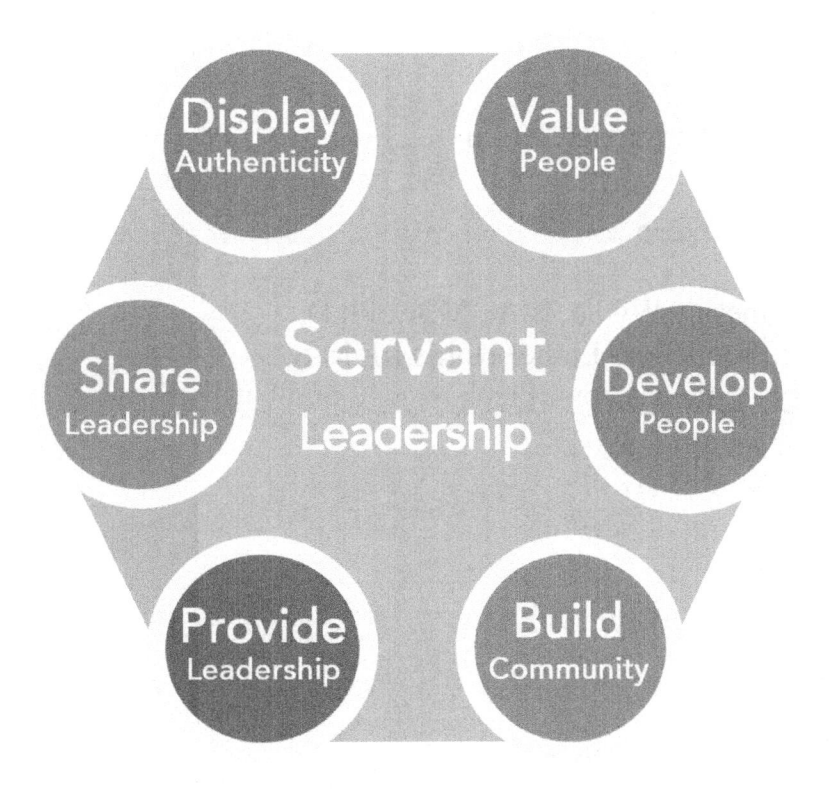

James Laub, Ed.D.

ServantLeader
Performance

Copyright © 2017 by James A. Laub | Servant Leader Performance

All rights reserved. This book or any portion thereof may not be reproduced or used in any manner whatsoever without the express written permission of the publisher except for the use of brief quotations in a book review.

Printed in the United States of America

James A. Laub
Servant Leader Performance
18240 Lake Bend Drive
Jupiter, Florida 33458
www.ServantLeaderPerformance.com

ISBN-13: 978-1981592357

Copy Editor: Katherine Wyma, B.A., M.A., Ph.D.
Book Design & Production: Luther Hollis III, M.S.
Images courtesy of: Pexels.com, Pixabay.com, and Unsplash.com
Images edited in Canva.com

For Barbara,
who faithfully models
leading through serving.

Contents

Introduction – Getting Started	6
Servant Leadership - Introduction (Day 1-5)	9
Define Servant Leadership (Day 1)	10
Learn the OLA Servant Leadership Model (Day 2)	13
Develop a Different Perspective on You as a Leader (Day 3)	16
Develop a Different Perspective on Those you Lead (Day 4)	19
Develop a Different Perspective on the Outcome of Leading (Day 5)	22
Display Authenticity (Day 6-12)	25
Make it Real (Day 6)	26
Build Personal Integrity (Day 7)	29
Become More Trustworthy (Day 8)	32
Be More Open & Transparent (Day 9)	35
Make Yourself Accountable to Others (Day 10)	38
Learn from Others (Day 11)	41
Develop a Humble Spirit (Day 12)	44
Value People (Day 13-17)	47
Put Others First (Day 13)	48
Believe in Others (Day 14)	51
Trust in Others (Day 15)	54
Listen Receptively, Non-judgmentally (Day 16)	57
Serve Others First (Day 17)	60
Develop People (Day 18-22)	63
Allow Others to Grow (Day 18)	64
Develop a Learning Mindset (Day 19)	67
Provide Opportunities for Learning (Day 20)	70
Model Appropriate Behavior (Day 21)	73
Encourage Others (Day 22)	76

Build Community (Day 23-27) — 79
Build a Team of Leaders (Day 23) — 80
Create Strong Relationships (Day 24) — 83
Work Collaboratively (Day 25) — 86
Value Individual Differences (Day 26) — 89
Build Effective Teams (Day 27) — 92

Provide Leadership (Day 28-32) — 95
Lead with Courage (Day 28) — 96
Envision a Better Future (Day 29) — 99
Exhibit a Bias for Action (Day 30) — 102
Display courage over fear (Day 31) — 105
Mobilize Others to Action (Day 32) — 108

Share Leadership (Day 33-37) — 111
Empower Others to Lead (Day 33) — 112
Facilitate a Shared Vision (Day 34) — 115
Share Decision Making (Day 35) — 118
Share Power (Day 36) — 121
Share Status and Privilege (Day 37) — 124

Servant Leadership – Conclusion (Day 38-40) — 127
Commit to Servant Leadership (Day 38) — 128
Develop a Mindset of Servant Leadership (Day 39) — 131
Increase the Competencies of Servant Leadership (Day 40) — 134

Conclusion - Final Thoughts — 137

Additional Tools from Servant Leadership Performance — 139

About the Author — 141

Introduction
Getting Started

Servant leaders do not lead by forcing themselves on others; they invite others to join them on a journey, and that is what this workbook is all about. A journey of change. A journey of discovery. A journey of growing as a servant leader. How does someone change? Changing into a servant leader requires addressing both **Attitude** and **Action**; how we think and how we behave. The change can be initiated from either direction. It can begin with a shift in our perspective; a different way of seeing the world. As our attitude changes then our actions often follow, but we also can begin the change with our behavior, by practicing what we want to become. Do it often enough and it becomes a habit—a way of being. And, your beliefs and attitudes will follow. So, this workbook comes at change from both directions, challenging our mindset (beliefs) about leadership as well our actions (behavior).

Will 40 days provide enough time to really change to build a new set of leadership practices? We know that becoming a servant leader requires a lifetime of commitment, learning and faithful action. But, 40 days of focus will go a long way to challenge our long-held beliefs about leadership that undermine our desire to lead as a servant. 40 days of practice will begin the process of habit-change that will initiate this metamorphosis from a limited self-focused leader to an effective servant leader. Whether you do this as a 40-day exercise or a 40-week experiment, just know that the learning will be intense but the rewards beyond measure. As you have heard before, nothing really worth doing is easy, but real change is possible and a new way of leading is within reach.

James Laub, Ed.D.

How to get the most out of this workbook:

1. **Read ... Think ... Act**
   First complete the daily reading then spend some time reflecting. Use the personal questions to think deeply about your own leadership. Use the Group Reflection questions to discuss with others on your leadership team who may connect on this journey with you. But don't leave this at an exchange of words. Act. Ideas for action are provided each day, so commit to doing one servant leadership action each day that will begin to improve your leadership practice.

2. **Reflect .... Write ... Review**
   Your workbook, for each day, provides space for you to write your thoughts, questions, and plans, so spend just a few minutes each day reflecting on new insights. Write down your thoughts to capture your learning in process. Then review the experiences of each day and the results of putting your learning into action.

3. **Interact ... Share ... Collaborate**
   Leadership always begins with the individual, but it is fulfilled within community. Learning is a change of thinking and behavior and that is best done with others learning alongside. So interact with others on this journey; share your thoughts and questions; collaborate in creating a new leadership practice for you and those you lead.

I wish you all the best as you begin on this path of servant leadership development.

Enjoy the journey.

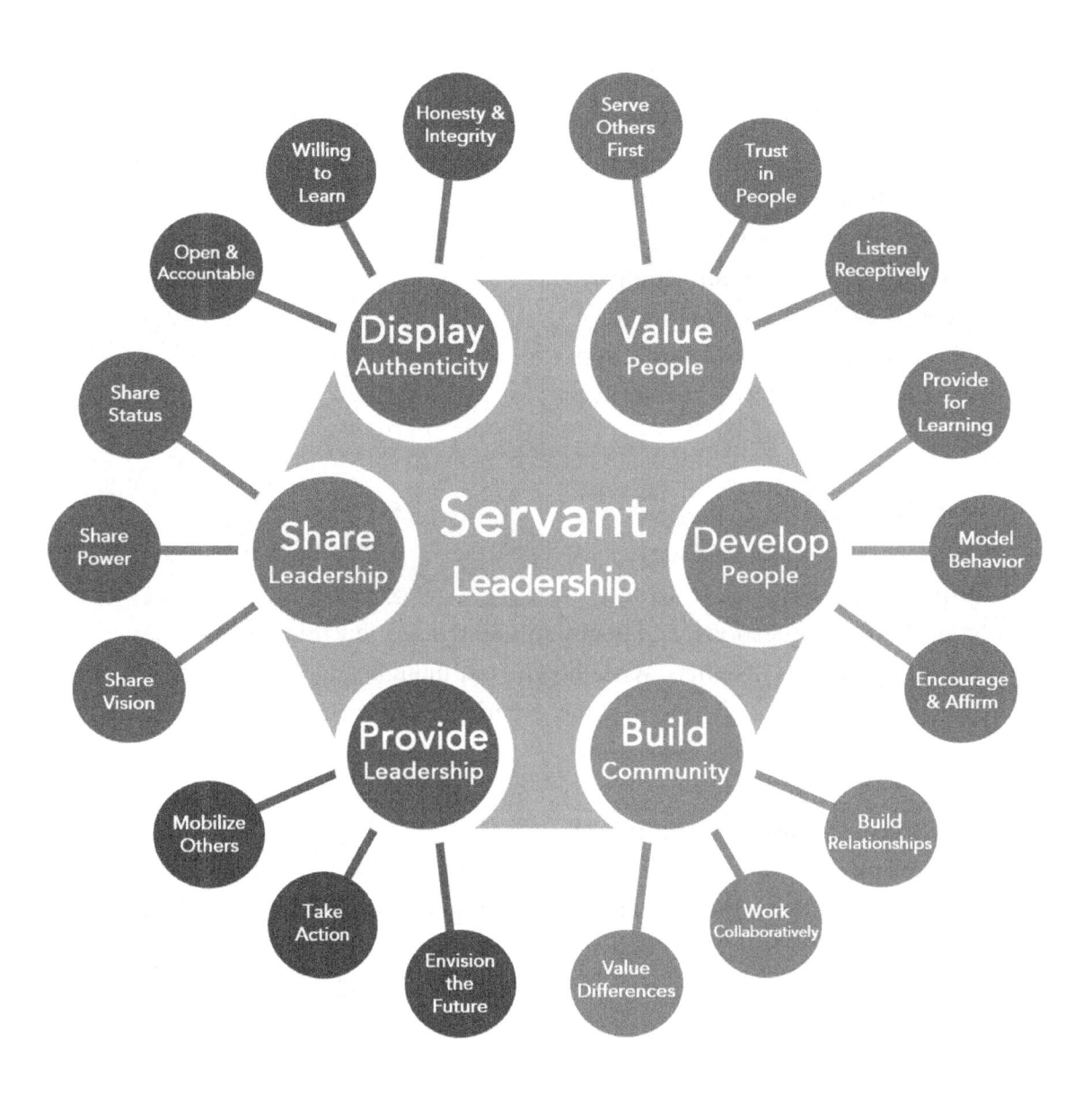

Servant Leadership

- **Display Authenticity**
  - Willing to Learn
  - Honesty & Integrity
  - Open & Accountable
- **Value People**
  - Serve Others First
  - Trust in People
  - Listen Receptively
- **Develop People**
  - Provide for Learning
  - Model Behavior
  - Encourage & Affirm
- **Build Community**
  - Build Relationships
  - Work Collaboratively
  - Value Differences
- **Provide Leadership**
  - Envision the Future
  - Take Action
  - Mobilize Others
- **Share Leadership**
  - Share Vision
  - Share Power
  - Share Status

Servant Leadership
Introduction (Day 1-5)

Your journey is guided by a definition and model of servant leadership that provides six key disciplines that we, as leaders, must develop first as a mindset and secondly as a set of consistent behaviors. These six disciplines are:

- Display Authenticity
- Value People
- Develop People
- Build Community
- Provide Leadership
- Share Leadership

It is through these disciplines that we display servant leadership to others. However, before we can consistently live out these behaviors in our leadership we must develop a mindset, a way of thinking, that will bring a different perspective on who we are as leaders; a different perspective on those we lead and a different perspective on the outcomes of leading.

Day 1

What is Servant Leadership?

Define Servant Leadership

What is servant leadership? These two words don't seem to fit together at first glance. Can you sense the tension between them as they audaciously suggest that you lead others ... by *serving* them? What does it mean?

Here's a definition for your consideration.

Think about this.

Servant leadership is an understanding and practice of leadership that places the good of those led over the self-interest of the leader. Now, let's take that apart a bit. Servant leadership is a way of leading that is distinct from other ways of leading.

Remember Machiavelli? This writer/consultant from the 15th century suggested that leadership is not about serving (he would have been appalled at the thought), but that leadership is about keeping the power of the leader first and foremost so that the leader always remains the most important consideration. Machiavelli believed that you should protect your leadership position at all cost--use your power to get things done because it is far better to be feared than loved.

Machiavelli's message is alive and well today, isn't it? His name has become synonymous with the powerful, heroic leader who bows to no one: the leader who inspires respect and, yes, even fear. We admire these leaders while being careful to keep our distance. But servant leadership is about focusing on our followers, our employees, those we lead. Servant leadership is the only approach to leadership that recognizes the negative power of the self-interest of the leader; that leadership power can be used for good, but it often corrupts the one using it. Servant leadership intentionally places the good of those led over the self-interest of the leader. Our focus is to be on those we lead, not on protecting our leadership position.

Today reflect on how you view leadership and whether you are closer to the servant leadership model or the one made famous by Machiavelli.

The choice is yours.

Personal Reflection

- In what ways is my leadership about me and my self-interest?

- Do I focus more on my needs or on the needs of those I lead?

- If I were to work for the "good" of those I lead, what would that look like?

Group Reflection

- How can we together develop a more servant-minded approach to our leadership?

- What can we do to build up those that we lead?

- What is the biggest challenge to making servant leadership work in our organization?

Practice – Action steps

- Write out a definition of what servant leadership looks like when applied to your organization.

- Share this definition with others and get their feedback.

- Identify leaders you have known who lived out the Machiavelli code. What did this way of leading produce in the followers?

Day 2

What does the Servant Leader look like?

Learn the OLA Servant Leadership Model

If someone observed you throughout your day today, what would he or she see? What would he or she report? Are there observable behaviors that would identify you as a servant leader? What does the servant leader look like in action? Well, certainly servant leaders come in all shapes, sizes, personalities and gift-sets. But, there are some common characteristics that your observer could note that would clearly identify you as a servant leader. For instance, in your conversations and actions, are you **authentic**? Do you speak the truth? Are you open and transparent? Also, do you show that you **value** your workers, that they are more important to you than the job you have given them to do? Is your focus on **developing** your workers rather than using them?

People have incredible potential that we often miss until we begin focusing on possibilities for growth. Do you work to build **community** in your team? Is your work style characterized by collaboration or by fostering a negative, competitive spirit? Do people enjoy being on your team? Would your observer see you **providing leadership**? People need and desire direction, but they want to receive it from someone who is both caring and competent. People also want the opportunity to lead. Do you **share leadership** with them? Do you give them a chance to make important and meaningful decisions? What would your observer see today in your actions and in your speech?

As an aspiring servant leader, you can begin today to focus your attitudes and actions around these six critical aspects of servant leadership behavior. No, it's not easy, but yes, it can be done. This begins with a firm commitment to serve those that we lead and to change our thinking and our mindset about how we lead others.

Personal Reflection

- Which of these six areas of servant leadership do I find most difficult to exhibit? Why?

- Which of these am I strongest in? (Reflect on a time when you exhibited this servant leader characteristic)

- Think of a leader who exhibits these characteristics consistently. What is he or she like? In what ways can you learn from his or her example?

Group Reflection

- Are we authentic in how we speak to each other?

- Are we developing a stronger sense of community within our team?

- What would an observer say about us and our behaviors together?
  How much do our behaviors reflect servant leadership characteristics?

Practice – Action steps

- Select just one of the six areas of servant leadership and focus on it today.

- Determine one thing you can do to display this characteristic today.
  Do this one thing.

- Observe your workplace. Where do you see these characteristics of servant leadership displayed? Where are they clearly missing?

Day 3

Why am I a Leader?

Develop a Different Perspective on You as a Leader

Servant Leadership

Have you ever asked yourself this question: Why am I a leader? Why do I put up with all of this aggravation and stress? (Leading is not easy!) If you are totally honest, you probably will consider responses like: the prestige, the money, the recognition, the power. There are many reasons why people aspire to leadership and remain in positions of great influence. How would a servant leader respond to this question?

Remember, the focus of the servant leader is on the followers. You are most interested in their wellbeing and their growth and development as employees and as leaders. I know, the others things are important as well. We need money; we can use our influence to get good things accomplished, and we want to be leaders who change the world. But, remember, we need to be fully aware of the danger of our self-interest in leadership. Yes, we want to change the world; we want to make a difference, but if we are really honest there's a pretty strong dose of self-interest in our aspirations of leadership.

What keeps that self-interest in check? It is focusing on others. Servant leaders work for the good of those they lead. Yes, they focus on getting things done, which is important. And they work to fulfill the mission of their organization, which is essential. They often have high ideals of changing the world in meaningful ways, but if all of this is accomplished without serving the needs of those we lead, by helping them to become leaders, then we are not servant leaders. Today, consider why you lead. Consider what drives you to do what you do. And consider the simple message of servant leadership: to serve the good of those that you lead.

What a powerful challenge!

Personal Reflection

- Why am I a leader? What do I hope to gain from doing this?

- What is my priority focus as a leader? My followers or my personal goals?

- What is my central role as a leader? How can I act on that today?

Group Reflection

- In what ways does our self-interest get in the way of serving others?

- How can we better serve each other on this team?

- If we could change one thing to create more of a servant spirit here, what would it be?

Practice – Action steps

- Write down your legitimate self-interests related to your leadership role.

- Serve one of your workers today. Do something that will help them do their job better and easier.

- Ask your team to come up with a list of ideas of how to serve others within your organization.

Day 4

How Do I View My Followers?

Develop a Different Perspective on Those You Lead

Servant Leadership

In the mid-1950's Douglas MacGregor developed the singular theory he called Theory X/Theory Y. This theory suggests that leaders have a particular view of their followers; either a Theory X view or a Theory Y view. The Theory X view is that workers are basically lazy, need to be controlled and supervised closely, do not want to lead or take on responsibility and will cut corners in order to get out of work. Have you ever had workers that fit that description?

The Theory Y view is that workers desire to do good work and would rather be creative and accomplished in what they do each day. Workers, in this view, just need to be encouraged and allowed to do the good work that they really prefer to do. Have you ever had workers that fit the Theory Y description? Well, Theory X/Theory Y is not about identifying two different kinds of workers -- but rather two different ways that leaders *view* their workers. It has to do with the personal belief of the leader: what the leader believes about the people they lead. MacGregor goes on to suggest that the view we choose (based on what we believe about our workers) can determine how our workers will respond.

Do you remember the *Pygmalion Effect*? This is the change that occurs when people live up to the high expectations of others (or conversely, live down to negative expectations). If this theory is true (and many studies support it) then we as leaders have a huge effect on those we lead. Not just because we tell people what to do, but because we choose to believe the best about them. Servant leaders chose to adopt a Theory Y view of the people they lead. Sometimes against opposing evidence, the servant leader makes a choice to see the best in their workers, to believe in their potential not just in their most recent performance. How do you view your workers?

Personal Reflection

- When I think of my workers, do the characteristics of Theory X or Theory Y come to mind?

- What might happen if I adopted a Theory Y belief about my workers? What would this require of me?

- What might change in the behavior of my workers if I were to change my view of them?

Group Reflection

- When we talk about our workers is our talk mostly positive and hopeful or negative?

- What is *our* potential? As individual leaders? As a team?

- Are we realizing our potential as a team, as an organization?
  How can we apply a Theory Y perspective to this team?

Practice – Action steps

- Write up a list of the positive characteristics you see in your workers.

- Conduct a Mind Experiment - Identify one of your problem workers and see if you can shift your perspective on them (from a Theory X to a Theory Y view).

- Share one of these positive characteristics with this employee. Tell him or her that you see this characteristic and that you appreciate it.

Day 5

What is my Goal?

Develop a Different Perspective on the Outcome of Leading

One of the old definitions of leadership was "getting things done through others." Sounds OK, because certainly we, as leaders, want to get things done. But think about the underlying assumption within this definition. People are a means to an end. Getting things done (the things I want) is the focus and priority. In contrast, servant leaders work against the tendency to *use* people to meet our leadership goals. Now, of course, as leaders we need to create a vision, act toward that vision and mobilize others to join in the process. But, what if our vision is not just for the grand goal, but first and foremost for the development of the people we lead and serve?

What if our goal is to serve and, out of that service, see our leadership influence expand beyond our expectations? This truth reveals one of the strange paradoxes of servant leadership. When we focus on the good of those we lead, when our main goal is to serve, then our organization benefits, customers are served, and our mission is advanced. By redirecting the goal of our leadership to the good of those we lead, we create a dynamic of leadership potential through our influence on our followers. Followers become leaders themselves. The team becomes a team of leaders, not just a leader with a lot of people waiting to be told what to do.

The power within servant leadership is unleashed when we dare to see the goal of our leadership as being the good of those led. Today, do some serious reflection on the outcomes you hope to see from your leadership. This is a perspective shift and requires a different way of thinking about leadership.

"I don't know what your destiny will be, but one thing I know: the only ones among you who will be really happy are those who will have sought and found how to serve." – Albert Schweitzer

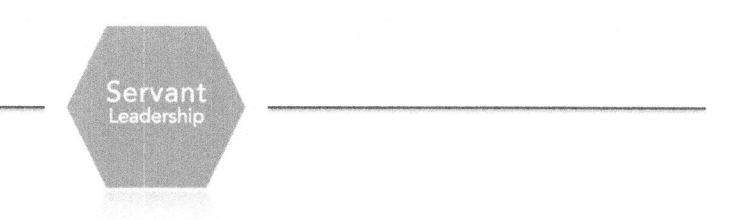

Personal Reflection

- How do I define my success as a leader? What will that success look like?

- When I think of my legacy as a leader, a parent, or a friend, what do I want that legacy to be?

- When I serve, how does that make me feel?

Group Reflection

- How do we get things done here without using people in a negative way?

- When people think of our organization, what is likely to come to their minds?

- Do *we* feel well served within this organization?

Practice – Action steps

- Practice gratitude – think through all of the things you are thankful for in your organization. Write them down.

- Tell two people today that you are thankful for their contribution to the organization (be specific in identifying that contribution).

- Identify three ways that you can promote a "people first" priority in and through your team.

Display Authenticity
(Day 6-12)

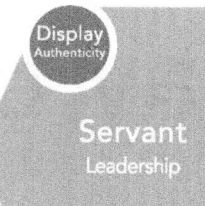

Servant leadership requires a different view of yourself as leader. You are to be open, real, approachable and accountable to others. You are not higher than others due to your position. In fact, position speaks to responsibility not value. As you work with people within your organization you will serve them if you display the qualities of Authenticity.

Open & Accountable

Resist the tendency to protect yourself at all cost. When you make mistakes … admit them. Recognize that you are accountable to others and not just those who are over you. A servant has nothing to prove and can fully risk being open with others.

Willing to Learn

Come to other people in the role of a learner. As a servant you know that you have much to learn and each person can be your teacher. You don't always know what is needed and what to do so you are willing to listen before making suggestions. Ask a lot of questions … and sincerely show interest in the answers.

Honesty & Integrity

Refuse to cut corners on the truth. When you make a promise do everything you can to fulfill it. People will learn they can trust what you say and that your actions fit your words.

Day 6

Servant Leaders Display Authenticity

Make it Real

Display Authenticity

What do you think about when you hear the word "authenticity"? Jim Kouzes and Barry Posner conducted extensive research involving multiple cultures, countries and languages. They wanted to know what workers want most from their leaders. They found that workers from various cultures differed on what they desired. Some wanted leaders to be visionary. Some wanted team builders … leaders who would relate well to them. Some wanted strength and confidence in their leaders. But they all agreed on one characteristic and it always came out at the top of each list. Honesty. Workers want leaders who are honest, who will tell them the truth.

This desire for integrity and truth-telling is global and unfortunately is too often missing within our organizations. A survey by A Maritz Research found that only 11% of managers were seen as backing up their word with action and only 7% of workers trusted their managers. 20% of workers had no faith in their leaders and did not feel their leaders could be trusted. Leaders without honesty, integrity and authenticity create an atmosphere of fear and mistrust. Some leaders are misled into thinking that fear is a useful motivation for getting people to do what they want (remember Machiavelli?). But fear only produces compliance and a weak commitment that produces very little for an organization.

Servant leaders are authentic. They can be trusted to tell the truth and to be transparent about who they are, what their motives are and how they intend to lead. There is an ethical and moral aspect to the servant leader that builds trust rather than fear, that encourages creativity and risk-taking rather than false agreement and avoidance. For these next few days you will be working on building an authentic mindset and authentic actions. You will work to build your character and integrity so that you can be trusted as a leader who is honest in word and action.

Personal Reflection

- When, recently, have I cut corners on the truth in order to protect myself and my leadership position?

- Do my workers know me? Do they feel that they can relate to me as a person as well as a leader?

- Am I honest with myself? Do I need to review my priority values and how well I am currently living up to them?

Group Reflection

- What is something we need to share with each other on our team?

- What is one struggle that each of us are facing now (at work and in our personal life)?

- In what ways are we failing to live up to our own values and beliefs?

Practice – Action steps

- Meet with 2-3 other people to share what is going on in your life. Share some challenges you are facing. What good things are going on that you are thankful for?

- Share with one other trusted person a struggle you are facing. Remember, a vice kept secret will control you. Be open and share this in an appropriate healthy way.

- Ask one of your workers what is going on in his or her life and share something about your life as well.

Day 7

Servant Leaders Display Authenticity

Build Personal Integrity

"Honesty is the first chapter of the book of wisdom." - Thomas Jefferson

Integrity, honesty, credibility. Are these words that come to mind when others think of you? Honesty is about telling the truth. Integrity is about having your actions match up with your words and beliefs. Credibility is what you possess when these two are in place in your life. Credibility is essential to developing workplaces where trust replaces fear and creativity is allowed to flourish.

Do you know how "Honest Abe" Lincoln got that name? It seems that in his earlier years he managed a country store. Lincoln was known to be honest, a great story teller and willing to go beyond the expected to serve his customers. Once when Lincoln was counting his cash at closing time, he discovered that he had taken a few cents more from a customer than necessary, so he closed the store and walked a long distance to return the money. Another time, he noticed that his measuring scales were off and he had given a woman too little tea for her money. Again, he weighed out the right amount and delivered it personally to her. "Honest Abe" didn't just speak the truth; he acted with honesty and

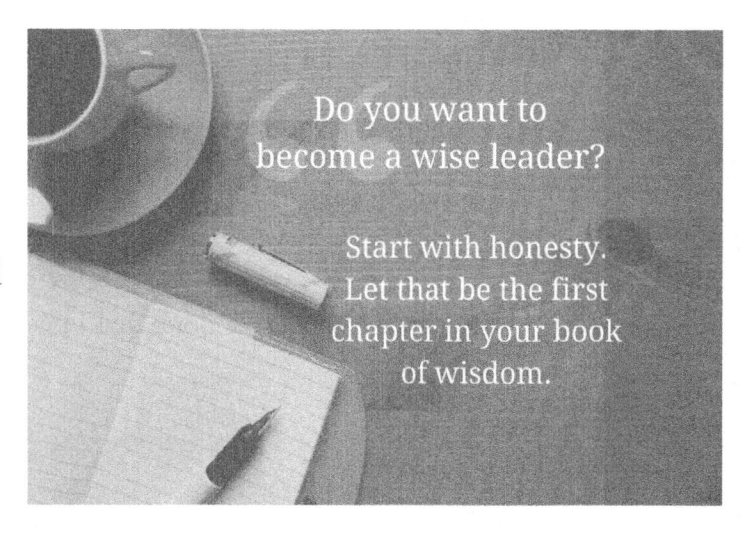

> Do you want to become a wise leader?
>
> Start with honesty. Let that be the first chapter in your book of wisdom.

integrity. If somehow he had wronged someone, he worked to make it right.

Servant leaders speak the truth. They refuse to cut corners or shade the truth especially when doing so works for their own benefit. Why? They are focused on the good of those they lead. Telling the truth, admitting a mistake, apologizing for a wrong done; these are very difficult to do and doing them shows great courage by the servant leader. Do you want to become a wise leader? Start with honesty. Let that be the first chapter in your book of wisdom.

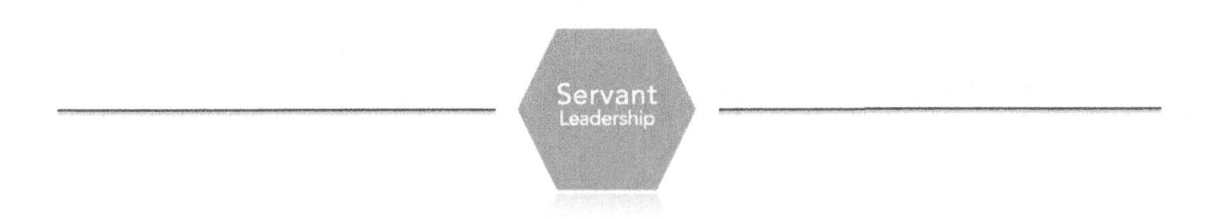

Personal Reflection

- When in the recent past have I been less than truthful with a colleague?

- What drives me to be dishonest? What keeps me from full and complete honesty?

- Is there a wrong I have done that I need to set right?

Group Reflection

- Is there anything that needs to be shared between us to set the record straight?

- Are we honest when speaking to our employees? Do they (should they) trust us?

- Is there an injustice or unfairness that needs to be made right? What would complete honesty require of us?

Practice – Action steps

- Based on your reflection time – act to make right a situation that needs to be addressed.

- Do an assessment of your team or organization to determine the levels of trust between leaders and followers.

- Create focus groups led by people your employees trust, to determine how they view the honesty, integrity levels within the organization.

Day 8

Servant Leaders Display Authenticity

Become More Trustworthy

What does it mean to be a trustworthy person, a trustworthy leader? Here are some definitions that you might think of: "able to be relied on to do or provide what is needed or right ... deserving of trust ... worthy of confidence ... dependable." In 2001 Kenneth Lay and Jeff Skillings got up before a meeting of Enron employees and encouraged them to buy stock in the company. Yes, there had been a rumor of problems, but the company, they assured everyone, was strong and returning to prominence. This was the time to buy, they said and many did. Why? Because they wanted to trust their leaders. They wanted to believe that the company was going to continue its incredible rise and they wanted to share in the rewards.

Unknown to the workers at that meeting, but fully known by those at the top of the organization, the Enron scandal was about to explode. In fact the leaders were selling off their stock at the same time they were encouraging workers to buy in. Enron's stock had increased 311% from the early 1990's to 1998. It then increased 56% in 1999 and then 87% in 2000. The stock price achieved a high of $90.75 per share in mid-2000 and then plummeted to less than $1 by the end of November, 2001. Workers not only lost their jobs as the company went down, but they also lost their life savings and financial security. Enron, Tyco, WorldCom. Each of these scandals has served to weaken the trust that workers had in their organizations and in their leaders.

Organizations need servant leaders to create a new level of trust, but we can't just tell people to trust us. We, as servant leaders, need to *be* trustworthy, dependable, worthy of trust. It is up to us to rebuild what has been lost.

Personal Reflection

- Do I trust the leaders in my organization? Why or why not?

- Am I trustworthy? Do I believe others trust me and my leadership?

- Do I trust my employees? Am I willing to give them the gift of my trust?

Group Reflection

- Do we trust each other?

- What would help to build trust within our team?

- Do our employees trust us to do the right thing? Can they depend on us to lead them well?

Practice – Action steps

- Be conscious today of telling the truth to those you work with.

- Consider a truth that needs to be told and tell that truth in the appropriate place.

Day 9

Servant Leaders Display Authenticity

Be More Open & Transparent

"Actually I think this is one of the most profound changes that more openness and transparency brings: it puts more weight and importance on building better social relationships and being more trustworthy" – Mark Zuckerberg

The common wisdom of past views of leadership was that the leader needed to maintain a distance from the worker. They were often put up on a pedestal and positioned above their workers (most top leaders still occupy the top floor offices). This created a safe place for the leader. When they needed to make difficult decisions (like letting people go) they could make these decisions easily. But abuses by leaders have opened up a new level of legislated transparency whereby leaders are accountable to regulatory bodies and new requirements for open information sharing. This new level of accountability is good and hopefully will lead to higher ethical performance.

But am I, as a leader, open and transparent with those I lead? Is there predictability in how I live out my values? Can my workers count on me to be consistent with them? Servant leaders are open and transparent. They comfortably and naturally communicate who they are and what their workers can expect from them. They are transparent with their emotions and reactions. Sometimes that can be displeasure and sometimes joy, but the servant leader is a "real" person, not a fake or manufactured image.

There is a whole industry around "image management" where leaders are taught how to appear the way they want to appear to others (stand a certain way to show command presence, hold your arms in a power position, hold your head up to show confidence). For the servant leader this is at best unnatural and at worst dishonest. I need to be who I am, not find new ways to pretend to be someone I am not. Servant leaders work on the inside issues (character, values, commitments) rather than creating new masks to hide the weakness within.

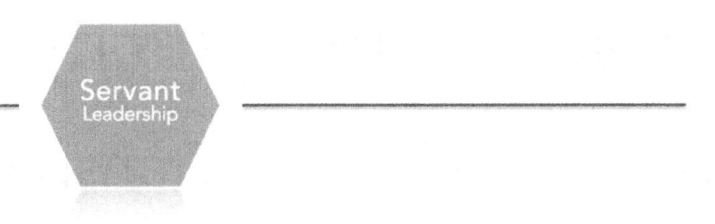

Personal Reflection

- Do my workers feel that I am open and transparent with them?

- Do my actions encourage others to be open and transparent with me?

- What is something I normally do not share that I could share to show a higher level of transparency?

Group Reflection

- How do we display ourselves as leaders to those we lead? How do they see us?

- What information do we normally not share that we *could* share to create a stronger sense of openness in our organization?

- How can we be more transparent with each other? With our employees?

Practice – Action steps

- Be open with your workers about a struggle you are facing. Let them see you as a real person.

- Share information with your workers today that will help them to see you as an open, transparent leader who trusts them with important information.

Day 10

Servant Leaders Display Authenticity

Make Yourself **Accountable** to Others

"Pity the leader caught between unloving critics and uncritical lovers"
– John Gardner

I guess if leaders had the choice they would much prefer uncritical lovers to unloving critics, but that would be a dangerous choice. Uncritical lovers (leader worshippers) certainly make us feel good, but they do nothing to help our leadership become more effective. At least our unloving critics (and we all have them) share their criticism and that criticism always contains a grain (or several grains) of truth. We need to hear what our unloving critics have to say.

Servant Leaders hold themselves accountable to others from all levels of the organization. Certainly we are accountable to those above us (that is required) but we also are accountable to those below us, those we lead. Why is it that we expect our followers to respond to our calls and emails immediately when we don't hold ourselves accountable in the same way to them? Servant leaders refuse this false standard and realize that a promise made to one's followers is as important as one made to one's supervisor.

Accountability. We all need it, but as we go higher in the organizational hierarchy, we receive less of it and seem to desire less of it. The authentic servant leader holds him or herself accountable for his or her actions and is willing to hold him or herself accountable to others; to both bosses *and* workers. Unloving critics or uncritical lovers? What if our organizations were full of loving critics? Maybe that would be the best and healthiest situation of all.

Day 10 | Make Yourself Accountable to Others

Personal Reflection

- When I have been criticized recently, what is the grain of truth that I need to accept within that criticism?

- What should I do to address this hard truth? How can learn from it and improve?

- Am I too captivated by uncritical lovers of my leadership? Do I seek feedback and accountability from others?

Group Reflection

- Are we held accountable for our actions, speech and performance in this organization?

- How might we enhance our levels of accountability?

- Who are we accountable to?

Practice – Action steps

- Ask your employees to hold you accountable for something you have agreed to do. Model through your actions your willingness to be accountable to others.

- Create one or two improvement goals based on criticism and feedback you have received.

- Ask for feedback on your performance as a leader. Use a 360 evaluation tool to seek input from those affected by your work and leadership

Day 11

Servant Leaders Display Authenticity

Learn from Others

Display Authenticity

Servant leaders are learners. They know they don't know everything and they have a deep desire to learn from others. This begins with two important considerations. First, you admit that others know more than you about certain things, and secondly acknowledge your desire to increase your learning. Learning is a habit, a passion and a discipline. To learn you read, you ask questions, you go to workshops, you put yourself in new situations to challenge your assumptions.

A wonderful example of this is the television show "Undercover Boss." In this show the CEO comes down from the top executive floors, puts on a worker's uniform and sees the organization from the viewpoint of the employees. This often leads to a realization of how limited his or her perspective has been. Top leaders have a very difficult time getting people to tell them the truth and that is a dangerous place for any leader to be. One of the leader's jobs, according to Max DePree, is to define reality and how can a leader do that if others are not willing to speak truth to power? The solution to this is to be a learner who is always seeking new information; presenting yourself as humble and eager to learn rather than the one who must know everything. The irony of all of this is that we, as leaders, believe that we need to appear knowledgeable about all areas of the business while our employees know that sometimes we do not know what they know. We need to learn from each other.

Servant leaders are learners. So, ask questions; not to test people but because you truly want to learn from them. Attend training sessions with your workers. Allow them to teach you. This will create the kind of open and learning environment that fosters creativity and risk-taking.

Personal Reflection

- What do you know well that you can teach others?

- What is an area you need to develop in? What can others teach you?

- What would you love to learn next?

Day 11 | Learn From Others

Group Reflection

- When mistakes are made are we more interested in assigning blame or identifying learning?

- What do we need to learn as a team? How can we best pursue that learning?

- Are we a learning organization? Do we continually learn new things, challenge our assumptions and expand our awareness?

Practice – Action steps

- Set a learning goal for yourself that will help you professionally.

- Set a learning goal for yourself that will expand you personally.

- When a mistake is made today, ask first what can be learned (rather than pointing fingers).

Day 12

Servant Leaders Display Authenticity

Develop a **Humble** Spirit

(Display Authenticity)

"To share your weakness is to make yourself vulnerable; to make yourself vulnerable is to show your strength." - Criss Jami

Every leader (unless you happen to be a narcissist) experiences the Imposter Syndrome. You fear that deep down below your mask of confidence that you really don't belong; that others know what they are doing but you don't. You fear that you are an imposter as a leader. Once, I asked the students in my class, the first class in a doctoral program in Leadership, which ones of them believed that everyone else belonged in this program, but they did not. All hands went up immediately. We all feel this way, and it is helpful to know that we are not alone.

As a leader I struggle with self-doubt and uncertainty, yet I feel I must hide it or others will lose confidence in me. This inauthentic situation can be a huge burden for leaders to carry. We know we don't know what to do sometimes, but we can't let on. We can't destroy the illusion that the leader knows all, or *should* know all. Well this is both the good news and the bad news of servant leadership.

Servant leaders can be honest and open about their failures and fears. Servant leaders can be humble and admit that they don't know it all and that they need others to help and support them. As servant leaders we can admit the truth, embrace the gifts of our team and see our weakness become the team's strength. The down side of this is that it's so humbling. There is something very appealing about standing high up on a leadership pedestal adored and feared by those who are dependent on us, but there is also something very dangerous about this kind of pride and arrogance that is so prevalent in leadership. Servant leaders are humble and because of that humility, can be incredibly effective.

Servant Leadership

Personal Reflection

- Do I convey a sense of humility as a leader? How might others see this?

- Do I come across as the expert on everything, or do I rely on the expertise of others? (even those I lead)

- Do I see humility as a positive attribute in a leader? Why, or why not?

Group Reflection

- Do we as leaders admit when we are wrong?

- Would we be more characterized by humility, confidence or arrogance? Why?

Practice – Action steps

- Ask your employees for their ideas on how to improve the workplace, or your leadership.

- Admit that you don't know something. Let others see your limitations.

- When you make a mistake admit it.

Value People
(Day 13-17)

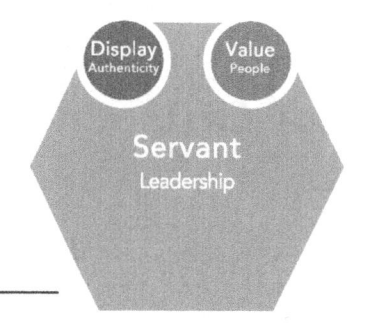

Servant leadership requires a different view of others. People are to be valued and developed not *used* for the purposes of the leader. As a leader I accept the fact that people have present value not just future potential. People seem to have an innate ability to know whether or not they are being valued. Whether or not they are trusted. As a servant leader we accept a person's value up front. We give them the gift of trust without requiring that they earn it first. As you work with people in organizations you will serve them if you display the qualities of Valuing People.

Serve others first

Put others before yourself. Focus on *their* needs and how you can best meet them.

Believe & Trust in people

Give them your trust. Believe that they can do the job. Envision their potential. Look beyond the immediate externals to find the true value of another.

Listen receptively

When we truly listen to another we will *hear* them if we listen non-judgmentally. We listen to learn … to understand. We listen because we know that it is one of the best ways to show that we value another.

Day 13

Servant Leaders Value People

Put Others First

"You can't lead the people, if you don't love the people. You can't save the people, if you won't serve the people" – Dr. Cornel West

Do you really value those you lead? I know you value what they do for you and the benefit they bring to the company. But, do you value them because of who they are as unique individuals and special creations of God?

People have inherent value, not just future potential. They long to be appreciated for who they are along with what they can contribute to the organization. Servant leaders are not afraid to use the "L" word when considering how they view their workers. Love. Tim Sanders says that "great leaders love their people." And, what does love demand of us? That we put the well-being of the other before our own interests.

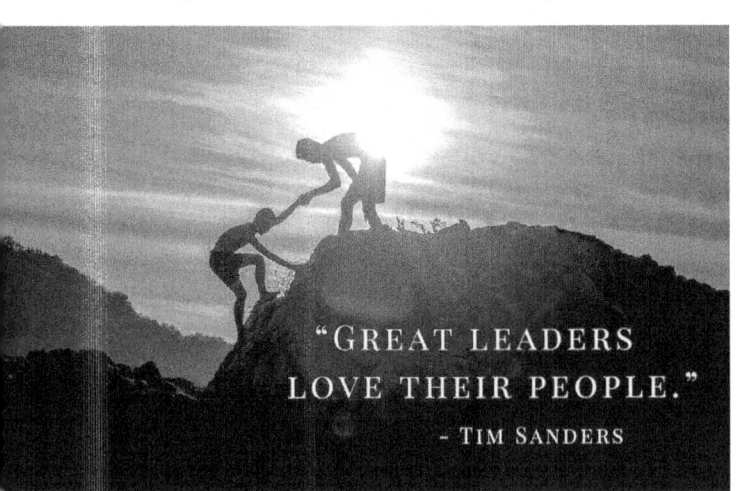

Love is all about serving. In fact, servanthood is love acting in life's relationships. It is love in action. When I serve another to truly seek his or her good, I am displaying love and the ability to love comes out of who I am. Tim Sanders stated "I love not because of who you are, but

Day 13 | Put Others First

because of who I am." I love and value others because that is a firm belief within. I serve because I am a servant. It is central to how I see my role in the world and in leadership. Do you really value those you lead?

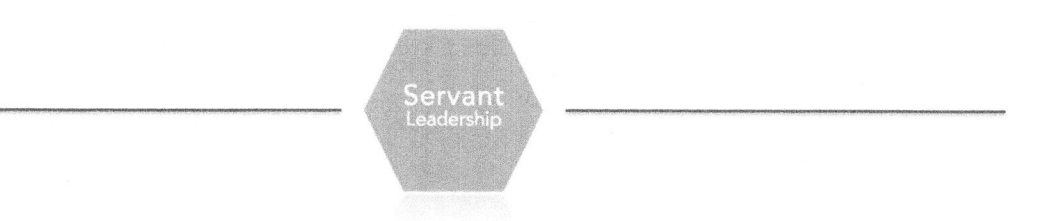

――――――――――――――― Servant Leadership ―――――――――――――――

Personal Reflection

- Do I value the people I lead, for who they are more than what they provide?

- How do I show them that I value them?

- Do I think of myself as a servant to those I lead?

Group Reflection

- Is love an accurate description of how we relate to each other in this organization?

- Do we show our love through service to those we lead?

Practice – Action steps

- Tell someone today that you value them, that he or she is important to you and to the company.

- Write down the different ways that your workers bring value to the organization.

Day 14

Servant Leaders Value People
Believe in Others

Value People

Have you ever had someone who believed in you *before* you had proven worthy of his or her trust? It may have been a parent, a teacher, coach or a boss; someone who had faith in you before you deserved it.

For me it was Ted Place, Executive Director of Youth for Christ (YFC) in Miami, Florida. I was a junior in high school, and I was a leader in the YFC club at my school. The club wasn't working very well and folded half-way through the year. Ted Place met me in the hallway of my high school one evening after one of our meetings. He looked me in the eye and stated with an amazing confidence "Jim, God has His hand on you. God is going to do something special through your life." Remember, I'm just a high school kid and I haven't shown anyone anything special yet. But, Ted Place spoke into my life a vision of something he saw that others could not see, and I remember it to this day.

Years later, after completing college I became the Executive Director of Miami YFC and, for several years, led the program Ted Place had begun. I have experienced the power of having someone believe in me and speak words of faith into my life *before* I earned them. Servant leaders value people by believing in them; seeing their potential and sharing a vision for what they can become.

Today, look at your employees, your followers with new eyes. See the possibilities, the potential that each one carries. See it and speak it into their lives and watch them rise to the challenge of your vision for their life.

Personal Reflection

- Think of a time when someone believed in you before you had proven yourself. What did this belief do in your life?

- Review the people you lead. What unrealized potential do you see?

- What is your vision for the people you lead? What can they become?

Group Reflection

- Do we tend to look more at current performance or future potential?

- How do we speak into the lives of our people in ways that encourage them to excel?

Practice – Action steps

- Speak into the life of one of your followers today. Share the potential you see for his or her life, work and leadership.

- Consider one of your workers who might be most responsive to being mentored by you. Begin to build into his or her life and leadership.

Day 15

Servant Leaders Value People

Trust in Others

Consider these two statements and choose the one that seems most true to you: 1) Trust is something you must earn, or 2) trust is something that you give as a gift. Which of these statements makes the most sense to you?

Now, consider the **Trust Game** developed by Joyce Berg, John Dikhaut and Kevin McCabe in 1995. The Trust Game pairs people randomly who do not know each other and communicate only through a computer connection. Each is paid a sum of money to participate. The first decision-maker (DM1) is told to send any amount they choose from their money to the other person (DM2) and that amount will be tripled in DM2's account. DM2 then has the opportunity to share whatever they would like back with DM1. There is no obligation to give any money back and both are aware of this. Do you see the trust issues involved?

If you were in this situation, what would you do? Would you give to benefit a stranger who may or may not give anything back in return? Interestingly, 75% of DM1's sent money to their partner and an even higher ratio of DM2's sent money back. A bit surprising, isn't it? Now let's go back to our statement choices. Did you choose "trust is something you must earn"? If so you are in good company, because most people make this choice.

Trust should be earned. But, servant leaders know that trust is something that should be given as a gift; that giving of trust to others creates a statement of faith for that person and most people will choose to rise up to the level of your trust. Give trust as a gift, giving it when you may receive nothing in return. Servant leadership is a risk to be sure, but a risk with a potentially powerful outcome.

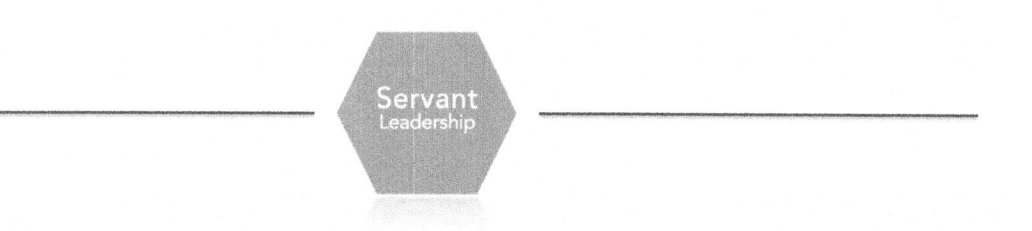

Personal Reflection

- Do I give money and talent to causes I believe in? Am I a giver?

- Do I give my time to my employees? Do I invest in them?

- Am I willing to give with no promise of a return?

Group Reflection

- In what ways do we as an organization give to our employees?

- What company policies could be reconsidered to make them more employee-friendly?

> Give trust as a gift, giving it when you may receive nothing in return.

Practice – Action steps

- Give something to one or more of your followers today. Give it freely with no expectation of a return.

- Decide to trust someone with a responsibility, someone you have been somewhat unsure about trusting. Tell them that you are giving them trust because you believe in them.

Day 16

Servant Leaders Value People

Listen Receptively, Non-judgmentally

Value People

"We must be silent before we can listen. We must listen before we can learn. We must learn before we can prepare. We must prepare before we can serve. We must serve before we can lead." – William Arthur Ward

Listening builds trust, pure and simple. When we listen, really listen to someone we communicate that he or she is valuable to us and have something valuable to contribute. But, when we listen it must be in a receptive, non-judgmental manner.

Have you ever spoken to someone who wouldn't even let you finish before beginning to speak over you, arguing a point? That person wasn't listening at all. He or she was just waiting to win an argument or put a personal opinion against yours. This isn't conversation, it's competition.

When leaders listen without judgment to their workers they set the stage to receive feedback they can't receive in any other way. Do you want to build trust with your followers? The first step is to listen to them. Even if you have limited time with someone, look that person in the eye, be totally present with that person and listen to what he or she has to say. Ask questions, seek understanding. People love to share and to feel that they are heard.

Also, people listen better to people who listen to them. Every leader wants followers who listen and understand them. Followers want that too. Servant leaders value people and show that value through receptive, nonjudgmental listening. It is the most cost effective method of trust building and learning you can have as a leader.

Today, listen to the people around you. Show them that you value them and what they have to say.

Personal Reflection

- Do I take the time to listen to my employees?

- Do they feel they have been heard by me?

- Do I ask questions that show true interest in learning from them?

Day 16 | Listen Receptively; Non-judgmentally

Group Reflection

- In our team meetings, do we really listen to each other or do we tend to talk over each other?

- Do we ask good questions of each other? Are we really interested in the other person's opinion?

Practice – Action steps

- Today, stop and listen to people you might normally rush by.

- Practice your listening skills (being present, making eye contact, asking good questions).

- Practice listening and asking before speaking. Listen fully.

Day 17

Servant Leaders Value People

Serve Others First

"Life is a place of service. Joy can be real only if people look upon their life as a service and have a definite object in life outside themselves and their personal happiness." – Leo Tolstoy

What happens when we serve others first before self? And, how easy is it to focus on others first? What about the ever-present power of self-interest? Adam Grant in his provocative book *Give and Take* presents three categories of people. Givers, Takers and Matchers.

It seems that some of us are natural Givers; we automatically give to others with nothing expected in return. It is as natural as breathing for Givers; they just live to give. Then there are Takers, who see life and relationships as competition and their goal is to always win, to always come out on top. But, most people, according to Grant, are Matchers.

Matchers look at life through a lens of fairness and justice. Matchers think, "I'll give to you, but I fully expect you to reciprocate." Grant has conducted experiments to test the motivation of giving. In one study within a hospital he set up two different signs at hand-washing stations. One sign said "Hand hygiene prevents you from catching diseases" (an appeal to self-interest) while the other sign said "Hand hygiene prevents patients from catching diseases" (an appeal to concern for others). Then Grant measured the amount of soap used by each sign. Doctors and nurses at the "concern for others/patients" sign used 45% more soap.

Day 17 | Serve Others First

Perhaps there is a stronger motivation than we normally think for giving to others over giving to self. Servant leaders serve others first before self. They strive to be givers who serve whether or not that service is reciprocated.

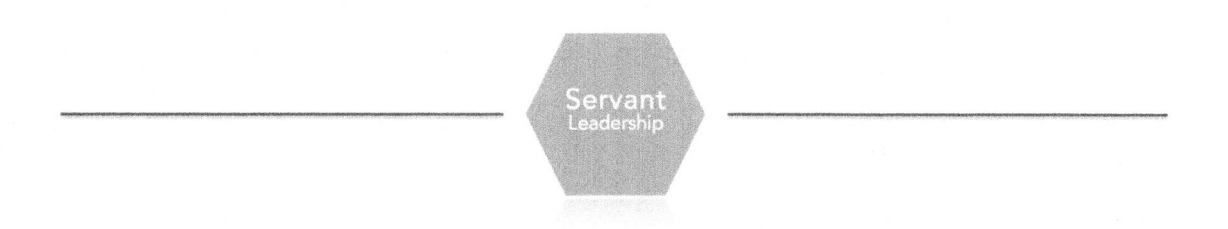

Personal Reflection

- Do I tend to serve others first or to serve myself first?

- Do I see myself as a Giver, a Taker or a Matcher?

- How could I focus more today on giving to others before myself?

Group Reflection

- Do we tend to motivate workers more through appeals to self-interest or giving to others?

- How can we create a more servant-first environment in our workplace?

Practice – Action steps

- Today, give to someone without any expectation.

- Give to someone in secret, so that he or she will never know it came from you.

Develop People
(Day 18-22)

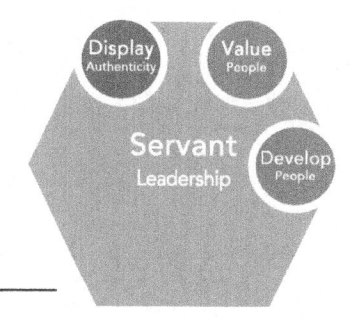

As servants we view the performance of others differently. Part of my responsibility is to help people to grow towards their potential as servants and leaders. Therefore, I am looking to create a dynamic learning environment that encourages growth and development. As I interact with others I am conscious of what our team is learning together. The mistakes of others are considered as opportunities to learn. We know that people have both present value *and* future potential. As leaders, we are part of helping them to realize that potential. As you work with people within organizations you will serve them if you display the qualities of Developing People.

Provide for learning

Offer people opportunities for new learning. Provide an atmosphere where mistakes can lead to new insights. Join them in learning.

Model appropriate behavior

Don't just *tell* others what to do. Model it for them and do it with them. We help people to develop by working alongside them so that they are able to learn from us … and with us.

Build up through affirmation

Encourage others … honor others … accept others … build up others. Catch others doing it right. Recognize accomplishments and celebrate creativity. Use words … let them *hear* you say words of encouragement. Be intentional with your affirmation.

Day 18

Servant Leaders *Develop People*

Allow Others to Grow

Develop People

"The most valuable 'currency' of any organization is the initiative and creativity of its members. Every leader has the solemn moral responsibility to develop these to the maximum in all his people. This is the leader's highest priority."
– W. Edwards Deming

Servant leaders develop people. Remember when leaders thought it was motivating to annually cut the lowest performers in the organization? It sort of made sense. Cut out the dead wood. Reward those who perform by allowing them to keep their jobs. Pit one person's performance against another's and may the best man win.

But, what happened in these organizations is that fear settled in like a thick fog. People would refuse to help each other or share necessary information. Collaboration went out the window; everything was seen as cut-throat competition. Yes, the highest "stars" were well rewarded, but many of these high performers found the oppressive atmosphere too much to take and they left to seek a more positive organizational culture.

Servant leaders choose not to motivate through threat or fear. They recognize that this kind of negative motivation only serves to weaken community, decrease risk taking and stifle creativity. Servant leaders want to see people developed to their full potential and are willing to invest in people. Why? Because they believe, value and love their people. They want to see them succeed, and this is the best attitude to develop to see your people flourish and prosper. And, if that happens, what might happen to the success of your organization? As a servant leader, provide for the growth of your followers. Find joy in their achievement and their professional and personal development.

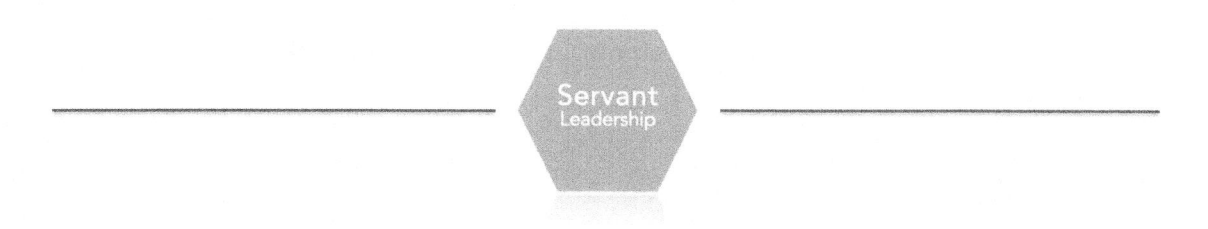

Personal Reflection

- Do I see my "highest priority" as developing the gifts and talents of those I lead?

- Am I learning new things? Am I committed to life-long learning and my own personal and professional development?

- Do I model a learning mindset to my followers?

Group Reflection

- Are we creating a true learning organization here? Do we encourage people to learn from mistakes and to try new things?

- Are we investing in our people? Money and time. Do they know that we are committed to their development?

Practice – Action steps

- List three things you would like to learn in the coming year.

- Set a plan to pursue at least one of these learning goals through taking a class online, reading, professional conference or in-company training program.

Day 19

Servant Leaders Develop People

Develop a Learning Mindset

How are mistakes dealt with in your organization? Far too many organizations see mistakes as failure and they feel the need to single out the ones responsible. This blaming and shaming reaction creates fear and uncertainty, and it does not work to create a healthy organization.

Consider the provocative actions of The University of Michigan Hospitals and Health System (UMHS). In 2001 they found themselves overwhelmed by the rising cost of medical malpractice litigation. In one year they were forced to pay out an incredible $18 million dollars in fighting or settling lawsuits; many of them over relatively small issues. How could they reduce their liability? UMHS like many organizations had a set of key values. These values were Respect, Compassion, Trust, Integrity and Leadership. But, unlike most organizations they really believed in these values, so they asked themselves "what *should* we be doing for our patients?" This led to a radical response to the high number of suits that involved less serious consequences.

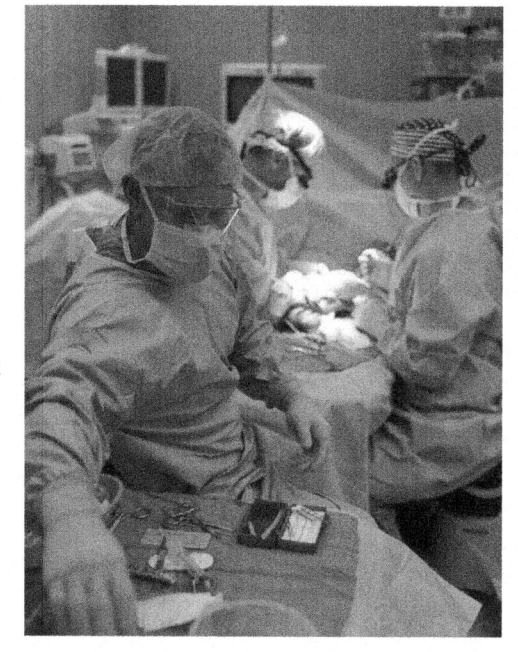

They encouraged their doctors and staff in these situations to say, "I'm sorry," to readily admit mistakes. What do you think? Is this legal suicide or honesty on steroids? Within three years of instituting this approach, medical malpractice claims and lawsuits *decreased* by nearly 50%. Clearly, people appreciated the honest approach and felt less need to pursue litigation. Servant leaders deal with mistakes with a learning mindset. Instead of becoming defensive, they admit to mistakes and resist the tendency to blame others.

Mistakes are part of living and working. The only way to avoid them is to do nothing. So, seek to learn from mistakes, your own and those of others.

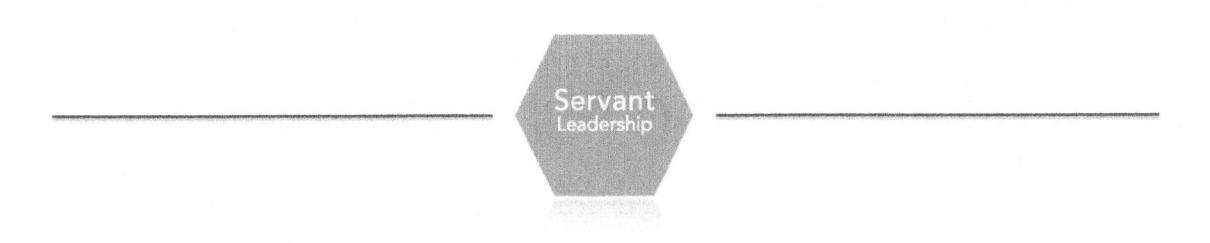

Personal Reflection

- How do I respond when I make a mistake? Do I seek to hide it or openly admit to it?

- What is my reaction when others make mistakes? Do I seek new learning or do I seek to blame?

- Do I view mistakes as an opportunity to learn?

Group Reflection

- Do we have a learning mindset within our team and organization?

- Do we see mistakes as opportunities for new learning? Do we talk openly together about mistakes from this perspective?

Practice – Action steps

- Consider a mistake you made recently and admit it openly. Model a learning mindset as you do so.

- Help your followers work through their own mistakes by drawing learning from them.

Day 20

Servant Leaders Develop People

Provide Opportunities for Learning

Develop People

"You gain strength, courage and confidence by every experience in which you really stop to look fear in the face. You must do the thing you think you cannot do."
- Eleanor Roosevelt

Why do servant leaders want to provide opportunities for learning and growth for their workers? Yes, employee learning can provide benefits for the company. Of course. But, for servant leaders it goes beyond clear and measurable benefits for their organization. Learning and development opportunities are made available so that each worker can seek to reach his or her potential, as a worker, a leader, and as a growing and healthy person.

We want to see our people develop and expand their abilities. Providing for learning is one of the most practical ways a servant leader can serve people. Give them a chance to learn something new. Give them a chance to develop new skills. Give them a chance to plan for their own learning so that they become life-long learners who are not satisfied to stay where they are.

Servant leaders are willing to push people to improve. They know that everything in life is designed to grow and the company will not advance beyond the learning level of its workers and leaders. So, encourage yourself and your followers to "do the thing you think you cannot do." Personal growth and development occurs within a balance of challenge and support. People need new challenges to pursue, and they need just the right amount of support to address those challenges. If the job creates too much challenge with not enough support, people will get disheartened. If the job provides high support but is not sufficiently challenging then people get bored and unmotivated.

Our job as servant leaders is to seek to provide a balance of challenge and support for our workers; to see them grow, to develop and to succeed.

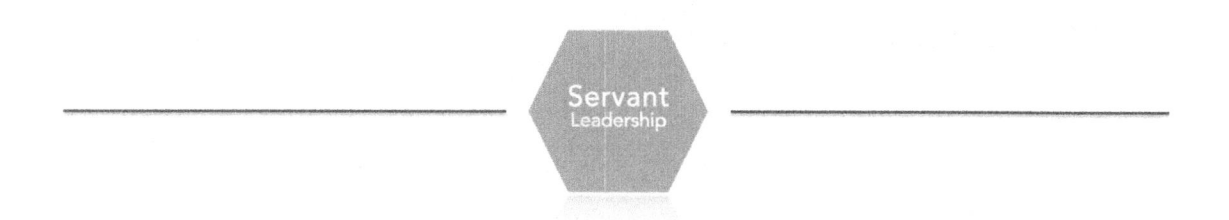

Personal Reflection

- Am I experiencing a balance between challenge and support in my work?

- How can I provide appropriate challenge to my workers along with the needed amount of support?

Group Reflection

- How can we create new opportunities for learning for our employees?

- How can we push ourselves to do more and learn more, to "do the thing you think you cannot do"?

Practice – Action steps

- Create an Individual Learning Plan to set learning goals and ways to pursue those goals.

- List multiple ways that learning can be provided. Consider in-company training, on-the-job training, volunteer community service and other cost-effective ways to provide learning opportunities to your workers.

Day 21

Servant Leaders Develop People

Model Appropriate Behavior

"Constituents pay more attention to the values we actually use (the values-in-use) than to those we say we believe in (the espoused values)." – Chris Argyris

In your organization, do leaders model the behavior they expect from their workers? Jim Kouzes and Barry Posner call this *Modeling the Way* and it is one of their five fundamental practices of exemplary leadership.

To illustrate this they tell the story of Les Cochran taking over as President at Youngstown State University. The university was located in the middle of a depressed neighborhood where gangs and crime were on the increase following the collapse of Youngstown's steel mill and the subsequent weakened economy. So the first thing president Cochran did was purchase an abandoned building on the edge of campus and then personally work alongside construction crews to build his new residence. He moved his family into the neighborhood, making a statement through action to support his commitment to the university and to the community.

He believed that a new attitude was needed; an attitude that rejected fear and hopelessness and the obvious decay around them. His new motto "Together we can make a difference" were great words, but the words now contained power and meaning supported by the new president's bold action. Kouzes and Posner state "While compelling words may be essential to lifting people's spirits, Cochan and other leaders know that constituents are more deeply moved by deeds."

Servant leaders model the behavior they expect and they see this as a central method for developing employees and building the values espoused for their organization.

Personal Reflection

- Am I willing to do the things I ask my employees to do?

- Do I consider some tasks as being *below* me, as OK for others, but not for someone in my position?

- Do I live out my personal values? In what way can this be seen by others?

Group Reflection

- What are our stated values as an organization?

- What values do we model before our workers?

- Do our behaviors as leaders match up with our stated values?

Practice – Action steps

- For each stated value of your company, list behaviors that will model these values before your workers.

- Consider focusing on one value each month and seeking to model that value through specific, and visible, action.

Day 22

Servant Leaders Develop People

Encourage Others

Develop People

"The first job of the leader is to define reality, the last job of the leaders is to say thank you. And in-between the leader is both a servant and a debtor"
– Max De Pree

We all need to hear words of encouragement and affirmation. Without them we cannot be sure we are doing a good job and that our work is appreciated. The servant leader knows that by giving words of encouragement we serve the need in others to have their work and presence validated.

All of us wonder at times; am I contributing anything of value? Do I matter? Am I important? A simple expression of gratitude goes a long way. "Thank you for being part of our team. Thank you for getting that job done for us. Thank you for coming up with that great idea." We need to hear words like these spoken. We need to go beyond the assumption that we are valued and to go beyond general statements that merely state that the leaders appreciate the workers. Non-specific statements like "our workers are our most valued asset" are nice, but not really affirming to the individual worker who wonders if he or she is truly valued within the organization.

So, do you want to increase the motivation of your workers? Do you want to bring out their creativity and ideas? Do you want to have them more engaged in their work? Tell them you appreciate them. Be specific in your encouragement. Tell them you appreciate them for (*add specifics here*). There is no financial cost to weigh; no budget category to reference. Encouragement is, by far, the most cost-

Day 22 | Encourage Others

effective, results-oriented action you can take as a leader. Today serve your employees by offering words of appreciation and encouragement.

Personal Reflection

- When was the last time I was encouraged or affirmed for my work here?

- When was the last time I offered words of encouragement to my followers?

Group Reflection

- How can we better show our appreciation of our workers?

- How can we better celebrate achievement and performance by our employees?

Practice – Action steps

- Walk around today and tell several people that you appreciate them and what they contribute to you and to the organization.

- Write a note of encouragement to one (or more) of your workers.

> Today serve your employees by offering words of appreciation and encouragement.

Build Community
(Day 23-27)

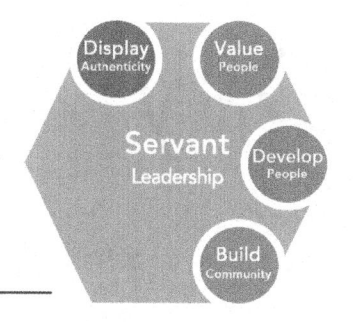

Servant leaders have a different way of looking at how people work together. They desire to build community, a sense that we are part of a loving, caring team with a shared goal to accomplish. We resist the tendency to "just get the job done." We are as concerned with the relationships of the people doing the job as we are in the job itself. We know that people will be more impacted by the quality of relationships than they will be by the accomplishment of tasks, therefore we will intentionally work to build a community that works together and learns to serve one other in the process. As you work with people within organizations you will serve them if you display the qualities of Building Community.

Build relationships

People need the time and space to be together ... to share, to listen, to reflect. They need to get to know one another. Don't encourage lone-ranger success over team accomplishment. Encourage friendships to emerge.

Work collaboratively

Don't allow the natural competitiveness between individuals to characterize the atmosphere of the group. We don't want to "win" at the expense of the team. Work alongside your workers and other leaders to model this kind of work.

Value differences

Respect and celebrate differences in ethnicity, gender, age and culture. Be aware of your own prejudices and biases. Confront them so that no individual or group feels less valued by your dealings with them.

Day 23

Servant Leaders Build Community

Build a Team of Leaders

"The leaders who work most effectively, it seems to me, never say 'I'. And that's not because they have trained themselves not to say 'I'. They don't think 'I'. They think 'we'; they think 'team'. They understand their job to be to make the team function. They accept responsibility and don't sidestep it, but 'we' gets the credit.... This is what creates trust, what enables you to get the task done." – Peter F. Drucker

The power of Team. The power of Community. The power of We. Leadership begins with the individual, but it is fulfilled within community. But, why are some teams characterized by commitment and loyalty while others are fighting each other and seeking to move the team in opposing directions?

Simon Sinek asked this question of a Marines Corps general who quickly replied: "Officers eat last." Following this comment, Sinek observed that when lining up in the chow hall, most junior Marines ate first while most senior Marines moved to the back of the line. The point sunk in. Officers in the marines are expected to put the needs of their troops ahead of their own needs and this creates a cohesive unit committed to each other and to their leader. What was being communicated here by officers eating last? The lesson is clear, the team comes first. This is the starting point for effective teams.

Day 23 | Build a Team of Leaders

Servant leaders are not satisfied to have teams that just get the work done. They want to see teams who build a deep sense of community (relationship + commitment) that transcends the task at hand and promotes the unique identity of the team. Servant leaders build community. They work to create a place that is safe, challenging and effective, and they do this by "eating last."

―――――――――――――― Servant Leadership ――――――――――――――

Personal Reflection

- Who were the most effective leaders in my life? What were their characteristics?

- Did these impacting leaders put themselves first or last?

- Do I tend to put myself first or last when dealing with my followers?

Group Reflection

- Are we an effective team?

- Have we created a strong sense of community among us and those we lead?

- How can we improve our community here?

Practice – Action steps

- Create a "leaders eat last" situation whereby the workers get served first and the leaders last.

- Evaluate your teams on two factors:
  1) getting results and 2) strong relationships.

  Are both in place?

Day 24

Servant Leaders Build Community

Create Strong Relationships

"There are many patterns, many beliefs out there about leadership, about people, about motivation, about human development. The essential truth I'm discovering right now is that when we are together, more becomes possible. When we are together, joy is available. In the midst of a world that is insane, that will continue to surprise us with new outrages in the midst of that future, the gift is each other. We have need for each other. We have a desire for each other, and more and more, I believe that if the real work is to stay together, then we are not only the best resource to move into this future—we are the only resource. We need to learn how to be together: that is the essential work of the servant leader" - Margaret Wheatley

"The gift is each other." What a wonderful phrase. Servant leaders work to build strong relationships at all levels of the organization. And what does it take to build strong, positive relationships? We grow relationship on shared values, shared experience and shared purpose. Leaders are positioned to provide all three. Work to communicate your values with your followers. Identify together those values that are shared and common to all. Create experiences that allow people to work together, talk together, laugh together and achieve together.

Clarify your purpose and make sure that purpose goes beyond just a profit for stock holders. Consider how each of the stakeholders within the organization (including your workers) is served by the organization's purpose.

Are employees a means to an end? Or is their growth and improvement one of the stated (and actual) purposes of the organization? Yes, "we need to learn how to be together: that is the essential work of the servant leader."

Personal Reflection

- Do I have strong and meaningful relationships with my followers?

- How can I, through shared values, shared experience and shared purpose, work to build these relationships?

Group Reflection

- How can we build stronger relationships within our leadership team?

- How can we build stronger relationships with those we lead?

Practice – Action steps

- Create a shared experience with your workers outside of the workplace (attend a sports or cultural event together, engage in a sport with your team, share a meal together).

- Work alongside your employees on a task to assist them, learn about their work and show your support for what they do.

Day 25

Servant Leaders
Build Community
Work Collaboratively

Build Community

"For to be free is not merely to cast off one's chains, but to live in a way that respects and enhances the freedom of others." – Nelson Mandela

Nelson Mandela, former President of South Africa, died on December 5, 2013, and a great leader was lost to the world. Before becoming President, Mandela was prisoner #46664 at Robben Island Prison where he spent 27 years of his life. When finally released, at age 71, he knew he had a choice to make. He stated, "As I walked out the door toward the gate that would lead to my freedom, I knew if I didn't leave my bitterness and hatred behind, I'd still be in prison."

Mandela made a conscious choice to forgive his oppressors and work toward the dismantling of the apartheid regime. Four years after walking out of that prison gate, he was elected South Africa's first black president and a miraculous transition from an authoritative regime to a democracy began. Mandela led South Africa away from minority white rule through an attitude of openness, reconciliation and forgiveness. But he did not act alone. Many know that Nelson Mandela won the 1993 Nobel Peace Prize for his leadership of a bloodless transition of power in South Africa, but most do not know that he did not win it alone. The Nobel Peace Prize was jointly awarded to Nelson Mandela and F.W. deKlerk, the former president of South Africa. Mandela and deKlerk were able to put aside decades of enmity to work together in partnership to create a new South Africa and the results were almost beyond belief.

Servant leaders work in collaboration with others and not just those who agree with them. They are willing to transcend disagreements and wrongs to find common ground even with former enemies for the good of the cause and the good of the people.

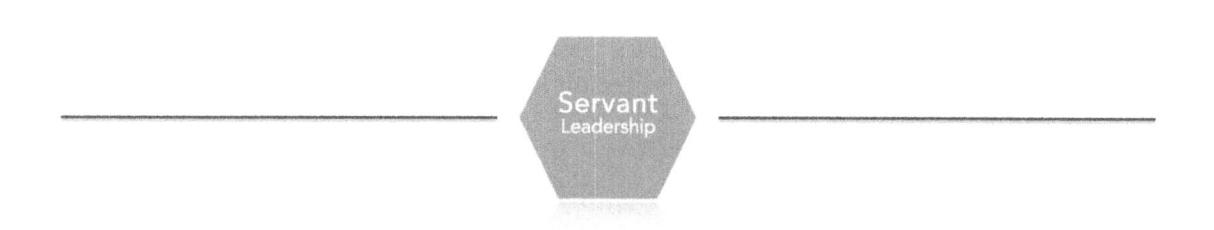

Personal Reflection

- Do I tend to work better alone or with others?

- Am I willing to partner with those who I have disagreed with in the past?

- What could I be doing more effectively through partnership than working on my own?

Group Reflection

- Do we have a culture that supports partnership and collaboration in our organization?

- Do we know how to work through disagreements to find common ground?

- Are we willing to forgive and create new ways of working together?

Practice – Action steps

- Connect today with someone you have been avoiding. Just say hello, ask a question, make a connection. Perhaps a renewed working relationship can begin.

- Ask one of your workers to partner with you on one of your projects. Ask for their ideas and don't forget to give them credit for their contribution.

Day 26

Servant Leaders Build Community

Value Individual Differences

"Strength lies in differences, not in similarities" – Stephen R. Covey

Our similarities bring comfort to the workplace. We like to be around people who look like us, act like us and think like us. But we need to be willing to go beyond mere comfort in the workplace. We need to recognize differences, appreciate differences and celebrate differences if we are going to fulfill our potential strength as a community. What might be possible if we blend together our differences to create something new and vibrant?

> *"There are not more than five musical notes, yet the combinations of these five give rise to more melodies than can ever be heard.*
>
> *There are not more than five primary colors, yet in combination they produce more hues than can ever been seen.*
>
> *There are not more than five cardinal tastes, yet combinations of them yield more flavors than can ever be tasted."*
> – Sun Tzu, *The Art of War*

In writing about how to be successful in battle, Sun Tzu recognized that the strongest army was made up of diverse individuals who when brought together could create something more powerful than the mere sum of the individual parts. An army, a team or a community of workers is made up of variety, diversity and opposing ideas.

As servant leaders we embrace this paradox, that the most unified team is the one that recognizes and celebrates its dis-similarities. Servant leaders build community by valuing and appreciating individual differences, differences of personality, gender, race, nationality, opinion and belief; a community that mixes all of the musical notes, the primary colors and tastes to create something new, effective and powerful.

Personal Reflection

- Do I tend to see those who are different as a threat or a valuable resource?

- Do I intentionally bring people together who disagree and maybe rub each other the wrong way?

- Am I aware of my own prejudices and biases that limit my acceptance of differences?

Group Reflection

Day 26 | Value Individual Differences

- How can we maximize the differences within our leadership team?

- Are we OK with the tension that comes from diversity?

- How can we build stronger teams that benefit from intentional diversity?

Practice – Action steps

- Utilize a personality assessment to reveal personality differences within your team. Seek to understand, and then appreciate these differences.

- Provide training to your teams to help them move beyond conflict to creativity.

Day 27

Servant Leaders Build Community

Build Effective Teams

"We had risen to probably one of the greatest challenges in history; put a man on the moon in the decade. We'd created incredible technologies. But what was most important, we'd created the teams, what I call the human factor"
- Eugene Kranz

"Hey, we've got a problem here." It was astronaut Jack Swigert speaking from the spacecraft Odyssey. An explosion had occurred two days into their trip to the moon and pressure in the oxygen tanks was decreasing rapidly. As the extent of the damage became clear the magnitude of the problem would test every leadership capability Eugene Kranz possessed.

Kranz was the Flight Director for the Apollo 13 mission; the leader in charge. He quickly realized that the solutions to the problem were not obvious and everyone would have to explore new approaches. And they didn't have much time. Kranz also knew that he didn't have the answers, but he was confident that his team did. They gathered in room #210 and began to identify the issues, create solutions and move forward to fix the problem. The lives of three astronauts, and the success of the mission, were at stake. Kranz spoke to his team. "Let's everybody keep cool. Let's solve the problem, and let's not make it any worse by guessing."

The team went to work creating ways to get the spacecraft onto the right trajectory to get back to earth. They solved the oxygen and electrical problems with very little margin to spare, and they were able to get all three astronauts back safely to earth. Krantz was a leader who believed in his team and the team process to solve the most difficult of problems in a very short time frame.

Servant Leaders know that they don't have all the answers. They know that all leaders have strengths and weaknesses, but that effective teams can compensate for a leader's weakness.

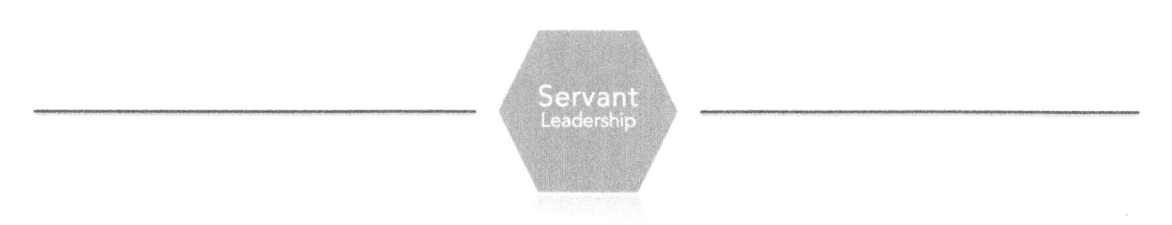

Personal Reflection

- Do I believe in my teams? Do I believe they can address the problems before them?

- How can I better prepare my followers to work effectively in teams?

- How can I better serve the needs of my teams?

Group Reflection

- Are we an effective leadership team?

- Do we trust each other and accept accountability to the team?

- Do we believe that teams can solve problems better than individuals?

Practice – Action steps

- Assess the effectiveness of your teams. Are their relationships strong and are they getting results?

- State your commitment and confidence in your teams. Let them know that you believe in their capabilities to handle the problems before them.

Provide Leadership
(Day 28-32)

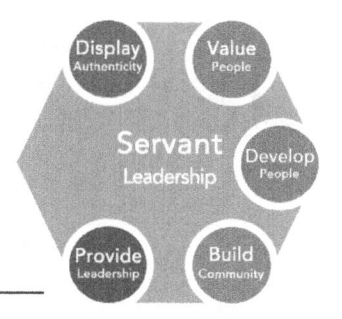

A servant leader *leads*, for the good of those being led. Leadership is defined through a leader's *Initiative, Influence and Impact*. The servant leader will not neglect to take appropriate action, in fact, leaders possess a bias for action. This initiative-taking comes not from being driven to personal ambition but by being called to serve the highest needs of others.

Envision the future

Leadership is future oriented. The leader looks ahead to envision what *could* be, and *should* be. Servant leaders recognize that they serve as partners with other leaders who also are looking ahead to the future. The servant leader shares their vision openly with the goal of creating a new shared vision with others.

Take initiative

Leadership takes action. It doesn't hold back in order to protect the leader from making mistakes. The servant leader moves out in order to serve others and to serve the agreed upon mission of the group.

Clarify goals

Leadership is clear on where it is going. The servant leader uses clear and open communication to point the direction that the group is committed to pursue. The leader encourages accountability to the goals set for themselves and for others.

Day 28

Servant Leaders Provide Leadership

Lead with Courage

"Courage is rightly esteemed the first of human qualities . . . because it is the quality which guarantees all others." – Winston Churchill

Servant leaders serve, yes, but servant leaders also lead and leadership takes courage and commitment. Leading begins with a **vision**; a mental image of a better future. As leaders we create the future by first seeing it in our mind's eye. It is an exercise of hope, faith and possibility. Then, once the vision is conceived, we must **act**.

This where courage comes in and it is in the action that leading actually begins. Anyone can dream. Anyone can talk about how things should be but it takes courage to act on a vision we believe in even when others may not be able to see what we see. Without action we merely have a dream and though the dream is the starting place, it really takes us nowhere without action. We must act in courage, never knowing for sure if we are right, but convinced that the vision must be pursued. But, we cannot act alone.

We must **mobilize** others to engage the vision with us; to help shape the vision and then act together to make the vision a reality. All of this, of course, leads us to **change**, the target and outcome of leadership. We lead in order to change the world by serving others. This then creates new leaders who work together to bring new vision and new change releasing a powerful, self-perpetuating cycle of leadership that can make our organizations so much more than they are.

Archimedes said "give me a lever long enough and a place to stand and I will move

Day 28 | Lead with Courage

the world." The purpose of leadership is to move the world, to move others to a better place. To serve a larger cause than ourselves. To serve.

——————————— Servant Leadership ———————————

Personal Reflection

- What is my vision for the future of my organization?

- Am I willing to do what it takes to pursue this vision?

- Do I have the courage and the will to act?

Group Reflection

- Are we developing a culture of leadership here? A place where everyone is encouraged to lead?

- Do we tend to have a bias for action? Or are we too easily immobilized by fear and uncertainty?

Practice – Action steps

- Write down your vision and share it to get feedback.

- Determine a courageous act that you have been delaying. Act on it today.

> WITHOUT ACTION WE JUST HAVE A DREAM AND THOUGH THE DREAM IS THE STARTING PLACE, IT REALLY TAKES US NOWHERE WITHOUT ACTION.

Day 29

Servant Leaders Provide Leadership

Envision a Better Future

"If you want to build a ship, don't drum up people together to collect wood and don't assign them tasks and work, but rather teach them to long for the endless immensity of the sea"- Antoine de Saint-Exupery

Servant leaders provide leadership by envisioning a better future. They are optimists who believe in others and seek to make things better for others. "No pessimist ever discovered the secrets of the stars, or sailed to an uncharted land, or opened a new heaven to the human spirit" stated Helen Keller, a person who knew that even a person blind from birth can envision a new heaven, that even someone without the gift of speech can lead others to an uncharted land.

It just takes an optimistic spirit and a willingness to dream big dreams. To be sure, a leader's vision is not always guided by a servant leadership mindset. A vision can be created for selfish or even evil purposes. But a servant leader sees the future through the lens of creating a better future for others. Servant leaders are not

"...a servant leader sees the future through the lens of creating a better future for others."

willing to sacrifice others on the altar of their personal vision. People are not a means to an end. They are not to be used to fulfill the leader's wishes.

The leader's challenge is not just to get people to do the work, to get tasks accomplished. Their challenge is to "teach them to long for the endless immensity of the sea." To *see* possibilities within the new vision. To see how life can be different and how hope can energize us to move forward toward change. Servant leaders provide leadership by envisioning a better future for those they lead and serve.

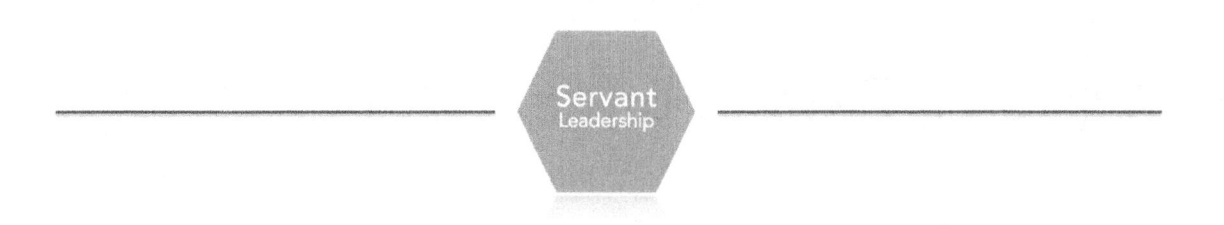

Personal Reflection

- How can I better communicate my leadership vision?

- In what way are others benefited by my vision?

- How can I best serve the vision while serving those that I lead?

Group Reflection

- What is the better future for our company? What does it look like?

- How can we motivate our workers to get excited about and aligned with this vision?

Practice – Action steps

- Ask your workers what they see as possibilities for the future of the organization.

- Create focus groups of your employees to collect their ideas and dreams for how the company can improve.

Day 30

Servant Leaders Provide Leadership

Exhibit a Bias for **Action**

Provide Leadership

One of the misconceptions about servant leadership is that it is weak, soft and not really about leadership at all. This is so far from the truth! In her wonderful book *Servants of the People*, Lea Williams tells the story of Fannie Lou Hamer, who during the Freedom Summer of 1962 decided that continuing to live in fear was no longer an option. She decided to take action to help the black citizens of Mississippi register to vote. In response to this action, she was evicted from her home, beaten and put in jail, but she could not be deterred. She crusaded throughout the state to address poverty, education needs and equal rights for blacks at a time when oppression was strong and the opposition fierce. She exemplified what Williams called "a rarer type" of leadership.

Williams states, "the servant-leader is committed to serving others through a cause, a crusade, a movement, a campaign with humanitarian, not materialistic, goals." Fannie Lou Hamer's favorite spiritual "This Little Light of Mine" became her theme song. She believed that the little light she gave could make a difference in the darkness of rural Mississippi. "I grew up believin' in God" she shared, "but I knew things was bad wrong, and I used to think, 'Let me have a chance, and whatever this is that's wrong in Mississippi, I'm gonna do somethin' about it."

Servant leaders lead. They have a bias for action. They bring their unique light and strength to a cause that is bigger than them, and they are willing to pay the price for this commitment. Servant leaders take action to pursue a vision and they make a difference, like Fannie Lou Hamer, for generations to come.

Day 30 | Exhibit a Bias for Action

Personal Reflection

- As a leader, do I have a bias for action?

- Where do I let my fear keep me from taking the action needed?

Group Reflection

- Are we action oriented? Do we go beyond discussion to decision and then to action?

- What keep us from acting boldly toward our vision?

"Servant leaders lead. They have a bias for action. *They bring their unique light and strength to a cause that is bigger than them,* and they are willing to pay the price for this commitment."

Practice – Action steps

- Take action today. Consider a specific action you have delayed unnecessarily, and do it today

- Consider how your actions will affect others around you. Act today in ways that serve the needs of those you lead.

Day 31

Servant Leaders Provide Leadership

Display Courage over Fear

"God did not give us a spirit of fear, but a spirit of power, of love and of self-discipline" – 2 Timothy 1:17 The Bible/NIV

One of the most action oriented presidents the United States has ever seen was Teddy Roosevelt. He lived a life of bold action. He was headstrong, courageous and sometime fool-hardy. But, there was no escaping his willingness to take on seemingly impossible projects, whether it was sailing the US fleet around the world or completing the Panama Canal.

In April 1910 in Paris, he gave a speech where he spoke of the "arena" of leadership and challenged his hearers to take on the challenge. Hear his words: **"It is not the critic who counts; not the man who points out how the strong man stumbles, or where the doer of deeds could have done them better. The credit belongs to the man who is actually in the arena, whose face is marred by dust and sweat and blood; who strives valiantly; who errs, who comes short again and again, . . . but who does actually strive to do the deeds; . . . who spends himself in a worthy cause; who at the best knows in the end the triumph of high achievement, and who at the worst, if he fails, at least fails while daring greatly, so that his place shall never be with those cold and timid souls who neither know victory nor defeat."**

Servant leaders lead. They do not simply agree to whatever their followers demand.

They are willing to enter the arena of leadership, take on the challenge and spend themselves in a worthy cause. Don't be misled that servant leaders are timid souls. Servant leadership is not the easy path. But, it is the most effective way to lead others by "daring greatly."

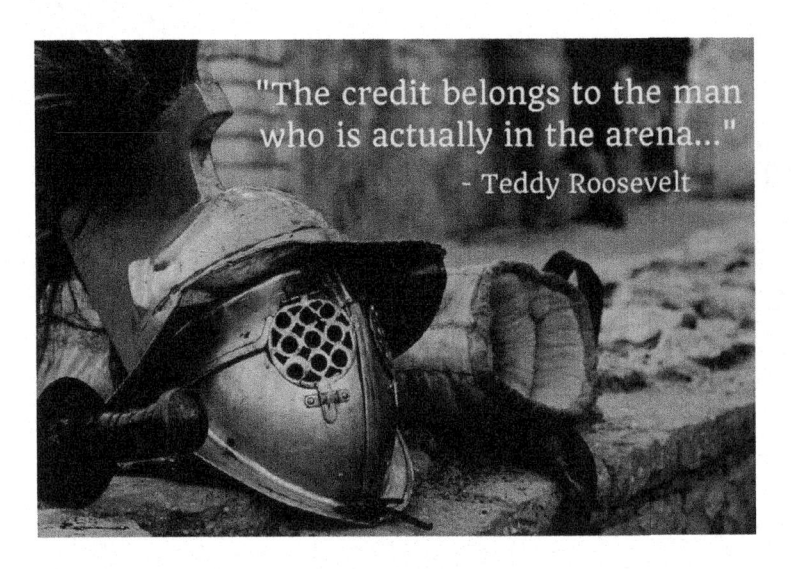

> "The credit belongs to the man who is actually in the arena..."
> - Teddy Roosevelt

Personal Reflection

- Am I willing to take a risk today? What is the challenge before me?

- Am I willing to "dare greatly"? Where have I been holding back in my leadership? Where do I need to enter the arena?

Group Reflection

- Are we reaching far enough with our vision? Or, have we been playing it safe?

- Where is fear keeping us from moving forward?

Practice – Action steps

- Do the thing you fear today. Find your courage in the act of leading in spite of your fear.

- Challenge your followers to "dare greatly." Model this for them.

Day 32

Servant Leaders Provide Leadership

Mobilize Others to Action

"What makes the temptation of power so seemingly irresistible? Maybe it is that power offers an easy substitute for the hard task of love." – Henri Nouwen

How do we motivate people to act? We know that power and authority works. If we have the power, we can order people to act and they will. This is, by far, the easiest way to get things done. But, what is the consequence of relying on power to motivate people? Power brings compliance and if that is all we are interested in, that is all we need. But our leadership should take our followers beyond mere compliance to true commitment. To get to true commitment, our followers need to know that we care for them.

The natural response to the use of force is resistance. So, when I seek to use my power and authority to coerce my followers to act, I am actually creating the resistance that will undercut my leadership efforts. We can't force people to buy into our vision or our values. But, we can create an environment where people know that they are loved and appreciated and then we can invite them to become part of the vision even allowing them to shape the vision. This is how the servant leader mobilizes others to join with the leader. This is how true and lasting change can be pursued.

Day 32 | Mobilize Others to Action

It is our choice, the easier and quickest way is to force our way onto others; to use the power we have to make them comply. Or, we can serve them, care for them, support them, allow them to become leaders alongside us and we will win not just their hands and feet but their hearts and minds as well.

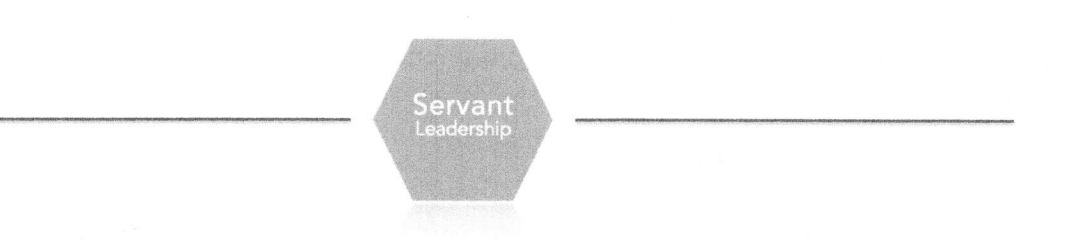

───────────────── Servant Leadership ─────────────────

Personal Reflection

- How do I motivate my followers to work toward their highest performance?

- Do I use my power and authority to serve the good of those I lead or to force compliance?

- Do I truly care about my followers and show this care to them?

Group Reflection

- Do our people feel cared for by us?

- Have we created a positive motivation environment or a negative one?

- Are we getting compliance or commitment from our employees?

Practice – Action steps

- Consider inviting people to take on a certain task rather than demanding that they do so. Let them know why they are needed and why they are being asked to take this on.

- Walk through one day evaluating how you use your power and how you display your love. Evaluate your learning at the end of the day.

Share Leadership
(Day 33-37)

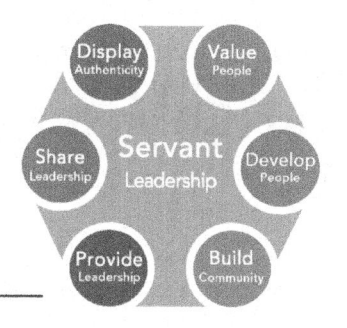

Every leader has power and must continually make choices as to how that power will be used. The servant leader shares the power they have with others so that they can lead, thus increasing the potential influence and impact of leadership.

Share the vision

The vision of a group does not belong to a single leader. A clear vision of the future shared by the entire group becomes a powerful magnet drawing together all of the resources, skills and abilities of the team. Vision comes to leaders who *see*, and a shared vision occurs when our individual vision aligns with others toward an agreed upon future.

Share the power

Power is the ability to *do* ... to act. In organizational terms it becomes the ability to make important decisions, allocate resources and move forward to make things happen. Shared leadership empowers all people to act, for the good of the group and the mission of the organization.

Share the status

Leadership is not position, status or prestige. Servant leaders resist the tendency to accept the special perks and privileges that come with leadership position. They know that all people need to be affirmed and recognized for their inherent value and for what they contribute to the success of the team.

Day 33

Servant Leaders Share Leadership

Empower Others to Lead

"A leader is best when people barely know he exists, when his work is done, his aim fulfilled, they will say: we did it ourselves." – Lao Tzu

I once conducted a workshop session with a counseling organization in Fort Wayne, Indiana. There were about 25 people in the session and we were going over their results on the Organizational Leadership Assessment (OLA). They had scored very high, Org[5] within the servant leadership level, and I wanted to see what this group was like in real life. So, I went in to my meeting with them as both a consultant and as an observer.

Here is what I noticed. First, there was a high comfort level in how the group interacted; a lot of humor, moving around, smiling and in general a positive buzz in the room—a sense of positive energy. Next I noticed that I could not tell who the leader was. The group met in an open meeting space with chairs and no tables. As people came in the chairs were claimed and informally shaped into a chaotic circle with no real definition or levels suggesting that anyone belonged in any particular seat. As most people were engaged in conversation a leader did not stand out

Day 33 | Empower Others to Lead

in any way. Then someone spoke up and the meeting began. "This must be the leader," I thought, but I was wrong. This was just someone who needed to share information with the group. Two or three other people shared before the CEO, a quiet but strong woman, finally spoke. She was not running the meeting, but was participating along with the group. She was present to learn along with the group and all were engaged in how they could become a more servant-oriented organization.

I was impressed with this clear and strong example of servant leadership, not just from the CEO, but also from the group as a whole. Servant leadership had permeated their organization and everyone seemed to sense the responsibility to speak, to share and to lead. Servant leaders share leadership, empowering others to lead until the organization as a whole displays these powerful characteristics.

Personal Reflection

- Do I allow others to lead? Or, do I always have to be in the #1 spot?

- Am I strong enough in my leadership that I can exercise it from a quieter, less prominent place?

- When should I step back and encourage others to speak out and take the lead?

Group Reflection

- Do we want to allow and encourage our employees to lead? Why or why not?

- Are we, as leaders, willing to follow and allow others to take the lead?

- Do we believe our followers have ideas we need to hear?

Practice – Action steps

- Become an "outside observer" of your group. What do you see?

- Ask someone from the outside to come in to observe your group in action. What do they see?

Day 34

Servant Leaders Share Leadership

Facilitate a Shared Vision

Share Leadership

"When people truly share a vision they are connected, bound together by a common aspiration. Personal visions derive their power from an individual's deep caring for the vision." – Peter Senge.

What do your workers, and you, care deeply about? Do you have a common aspiration for the future of your organization? Shared vision comes from the personal visions of each person brought together to shape a new vision for the group. If vision is dictated by management, the workers will not be able to connect to it and support it. Yes, the leaders must bring their own vision to the table, but they also must create safe places where the visions of the workers can be meshed into the larger vision.

Servant leaders are willing to share this creative power with their people. They are willing to let others create the future with them so that they can own this future together. This is the only way the team will have the passion to move forward boldly. Are you a forward-thinking leader? Research tells us that top executives spend no more than 3% of their time thinking about the future of their company. Do you suppose that is because we are so overwhelmed by the demands of each day that we lack the time in our lives to create the future? Vision is critical for leading and we need to give vision, communicate vision and share vision with our people.

Personal Reflection

- Do I know what my workers think about the future of the company?

- Does my vision align with those of my employees?

Group Reflection

- How can we create a safe place where our team members can share their vision?

- What is our vision as a leadership team for our organization and for those we lead and serve?

Practice – Action steps

- Conduct a retreat with your team. Allow them to share their ideas, thoughts, visions of what they see the company becoming.

- Meet informally with your workers one by one at different times of the workday. Ask them where they see the organization in a few years. Where *should* the organization be moving?

Day 35

Servant Leaders Share Leadership

Share Decision Making

Share Leadership

Bob Chapman is Chairman and CEO of Barry-Wehmiller Companies, Inc. a very successful company (20% growth per year since 1998) due to a clear focus on its people. The company slogan is "We build Great People." Chapman shared, in a recent TED Talk that seven out of eight people in the workforce today do not believe their company cares for them. He labels this a "crisis of leadership." Why? Because he believes that "everyone matters" and we need to help our workers discover their gifts, develop their gifts, share their gifts and then to be recognized for their gifts.

Barry-Wehmiller believes in validating the work of each individual by giving them a say in how the organization functions and how to better serve the customers. Chapman states "we've been paying people for their hands for years. We could have had their heads and their hearts for free if we had just asked for it." To get the worker's heads and hearts engaged, Barry-Wehmiller promotes what they call "truly human leadership" that focuses first on people, then on purpose and finally on performance.

Servant leaders recognize that we need more than just the hands of our workers. We need to engage their heads (their ideas) and their hearts (their commitment) as well. To do this we need to allow workers at all levels to make important decisions that matter to the employees and the customers. Hands + Heads + Hearts. Our workers bring all three to work, but have often not been encouraged to use them all fully for the good of the company.

Day 35 | Share Decision Making

The servant leader wants to share leadership with the followers by engaging them at every level and empowering them to make decisions that are important to the direction and success of the company.

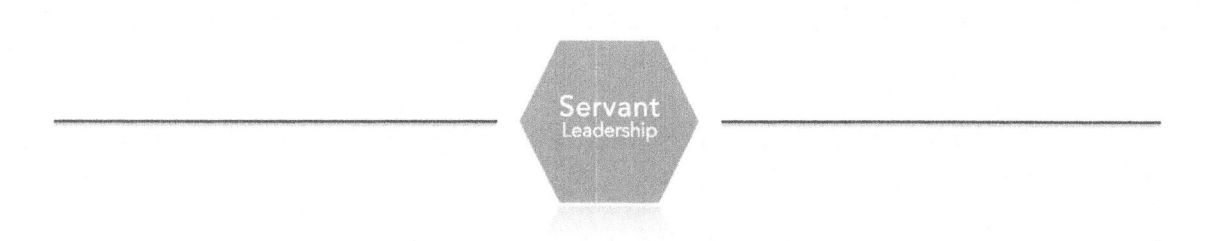

Personal Reflection

- What keeps me from being more comfortable delegating important decisions to my workers?

- How do I respond when someone places trust in me and values my ideas (head) and my commitment (heart)?

- Do I trust my workers to make more important decisions for the company?

Group Reflection

- What decisions would be better made by our workers rather than us?

- How can we push more decisions down to those who are doing the work and interacting directly with our customers?

- What training can be provided to better equip our employees to make these decisions?

Practice – Action steps

- Ask your workers what they think about specific important decisions. Really listen to what they are saying.

- Review the decision making grid for your organization – are the right people responsible for making the right decisions?

Day 36

Servant Leaders Share Leadership

Share Power

"As we look ahead into the next century, leaders will be those who empower others."
– Bill Gates

"Great leaders give control, they don't take control" – David Marquet

When David Marquet took over as Captain of the nuclear submarine *Santa Fe* it was the poorest performing sub in the fleet. Over the prior year David had studied the sub he was scheduled to take over and he knew the ship backwards and forwards, but at the very last minute, his assignment was changed to the *Santa Fe*. When he boarded as Captain he knew less about the ship than anyone else and he quickly realized how dependent he was on others. He tried to be the bold, commanding leader but he knew that wouldn't work for long. He knew how to command, but he didn't know the ship.

The officers under him knew the ship but only understood compliance to orders. This was a disaster waiting to happen.

Marquet gathered his men and told

them that they would all need to become leaders and do the jobs they were all trained to do. By allowing others to lead, he opened up their creativity and commitment to their jobs. People stepped up because they knew they needed to provide leadership and expertise, and only they could provide it. The sub moved from a commander with compliant followers to a team of leaders. No excuses, no blaming others; everyone was expected to lead. And lead they did. The *Santa Fe* moved from worst to first in the fleet in all categories and several of the officers ended up commanding nuclear subs in the future.

Servant leaders give away their power to others so that they can become more effective leaders. Giving away power is risky and some are not willing to take that risk. But, if David Marquet can find success in trusting others to lead on a nuclear submarine, perhaps you can trust your followers with more responsibility.

Personal Reflection

- How do I feel about sharing more power with those I lead?

- What might happen if I allowed others to exercise more power in decision making and problem solving?

Group Reflection

- Is the power to lead focused at the top of our organization or is it dispersed throughout the organization?

- How can we empower more people to exercise their power to take action to benefit our company?

Practice – Action steps

- Give away some of your power to others. This will not decrease the power you have but will multiply it through others.

- Allow your team leaders and their teams to have more say in the areas their team oversees. Consider allowing them to move from making recommendations to making decisions.

Day 37

Servant Leaders Share Leadership

Share Status and Privilege

Share Leadership

"To thrive as a servant-leader, you don't need symbols of success. You need to get material results for your organization, but you need spiritual returns for yourself. You need the personal meaning that will feed your spirit and your soul and give you deep happiness. You need the kind of happiness that cannot come from power, wealth, or fame. You need the happiness that can only come from a life of service"
- Kent Keith

Leaders have come to expect the special perks of leadership. With a leadership position we are given power, privilege and prestige, and it is hard not to accept these as our right. But, servant leaders work to share status, prestige and privilege with others. They seek the advancement of their workers more than for themselves. They hold lightly to the perks that leadership roles often bring so that they do not find themselves separate and removed from those they lead.

Consider practical things like reserved parking spaces, free meals, and office location, the things that people look at as symbols of success. Do we need them? Do they help to build community or to separate us from those on our team? Servant leaders are focused on serving the needs of others ahead of their own needs. They are aware of the symbols of power (like sitting at the head of the board table) and they work to push others ahead while intentionally holding themselves back. As a leader, share your leadership with others. Share the symbols of success with them.

Day 37 | Share Status and Privilege

Servant Leadership

Personal Reflection

- What are some of the perks of leadership that I enjoy?

- How might I share more power, status, prestige and privilege with those I lead?

Group Reflection

- How do we deal with symbols of success in our organization?

- How can we share these privileges more with those we lead?

Practice – Action steps

- Consider creating new symbols of success for your organization by creating ways to recognize leadership at all levels of the organization.

- Consider removing or redistributing some of the perks of leadership that may serve more to separate leaders from followers.

40 Days Toward a Servant Leader Mindset

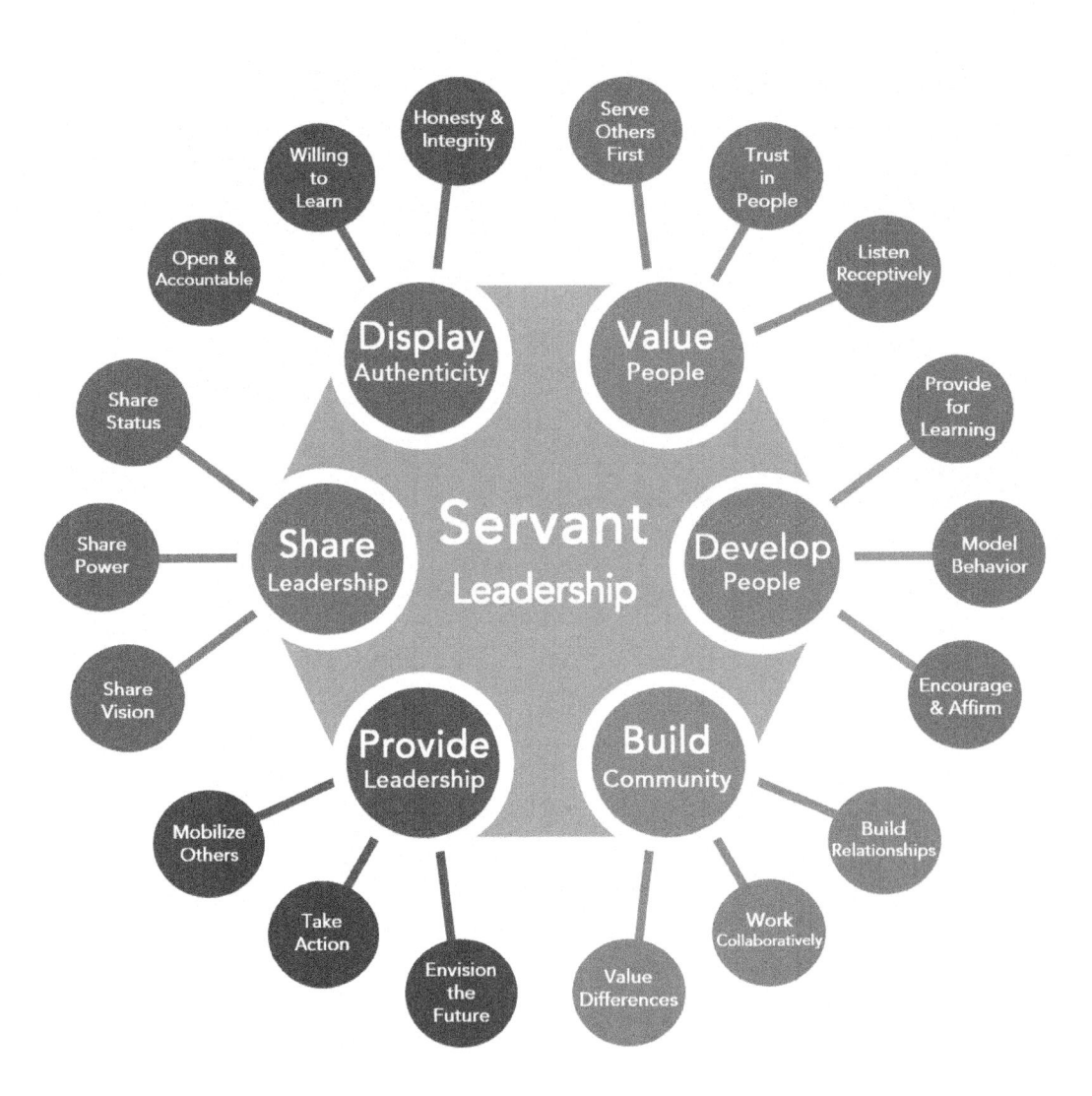

Servant Leadership

- **Display Authenticity**
  - Open & Accountable
  - Willing to Learn
  - Honesty & Integrity

- **Value People**
  - Serve Others First
  - Trust in People
  - Listen Receptively

- **Develop People**
  - Provide for Learning
  - Model Behavior
  - Encourage & Affirm

- **Build Community**
  - Build Relationships
  - Work Collaboratively
  - Value Differences

- **Provide Leadership**
  - Mobilize Others
  - Take Action
  - Envision the Future

- **Share Leadership**
  - Share Status
  - Share Power
  - Share Vision

Servant Leadership
Conclusion

As you end your 40 day journey, give consideration to the commitment you need to make as to *how* you will lead. Let this model be your guide as you work to consistently act according to the six disciplines of servant leadership.

Display Authenticity

Value People

Develop People

Build Community

Provide Leadership

Share Leadership

The servant leadership journey, of course, is a life-long pursuit, but it begins with a commitment to develop a mindset and build your competencies in servant leadership.

Day 38

This is Just the Beginning

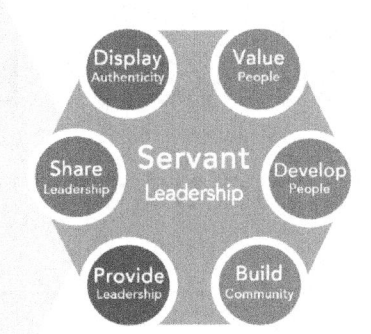

Commit to Servant Leadership

If you have gotten this far in the workbook, you are truly committed to improving yourself as a servant leader. But, you may still have the question. Does this stuff really work? Consider research conducted by James Sipe and Don Frick reported in their book *Seven Pillars of Servant Leadership: Practicing the Wisdom of Leading by Serving*. The authors compared the eleven companies evaluated by Jim Collins in his seminal "Good to Great" study (Fannie Mae, Circuit City, Nucor, Kroger, Walgreens, Wells Fargo, Altria Group, Gillette, Pitney Bowes, Kimberly Clark, Abbott Laboratories) with eleven companies recognized as being led by servant leaders (Toro Company, Southwest Airlines, Starbucks, AFLAC, Men's Wearhouse, Synovus Financial, Herman Miller, Service Masters, Marriott International, FedEx and Medtronic).

Here is what they found over a ten year period applying the same metrics used by Jim Collins:

- Stocks from the 500 largest public companies averaged a 10.8% return
- The companies studied by Jim Collins averaged a 17.5% return
- The servant-led companies averaged a 24.2% return

Let me share a caution here. We don't choose to walk the difficult path of servant leadership because we think it will bring us a big financial return; it may not. We do it because we believe it is the right way to lead and provides the best opportunity to

Day 39 | Develop a Mindset of Servant Leadership

develop those we lead. But, clearly, an organization that is well-led, healthy and is continually producing new leaders at all levels of the organization can be hugely successful as this study shows. Can you commit to servant leadership without hurting your company? Yes.

Personal Reflection

- Why do I pursue a servant leadership approach? Why is this important to me?

- Do I believe that this approach to leading will not hinder my organization, but will give it the best opportunity for success? Why?

- Am I committed to servant leadership?

Group Reflection

- Are we committed together to building a servant organization through servant leadership practice?

- What is the biggest obstacle to seeing this realized?

Practice – Action steps

- Identify actions to take in all six disciplines of servant leadership and plan to apply these actions over the next few months.

- Measure your employee perceptions along with the success of your company on key metrics of servant leadership. Consider how the OLA might help.

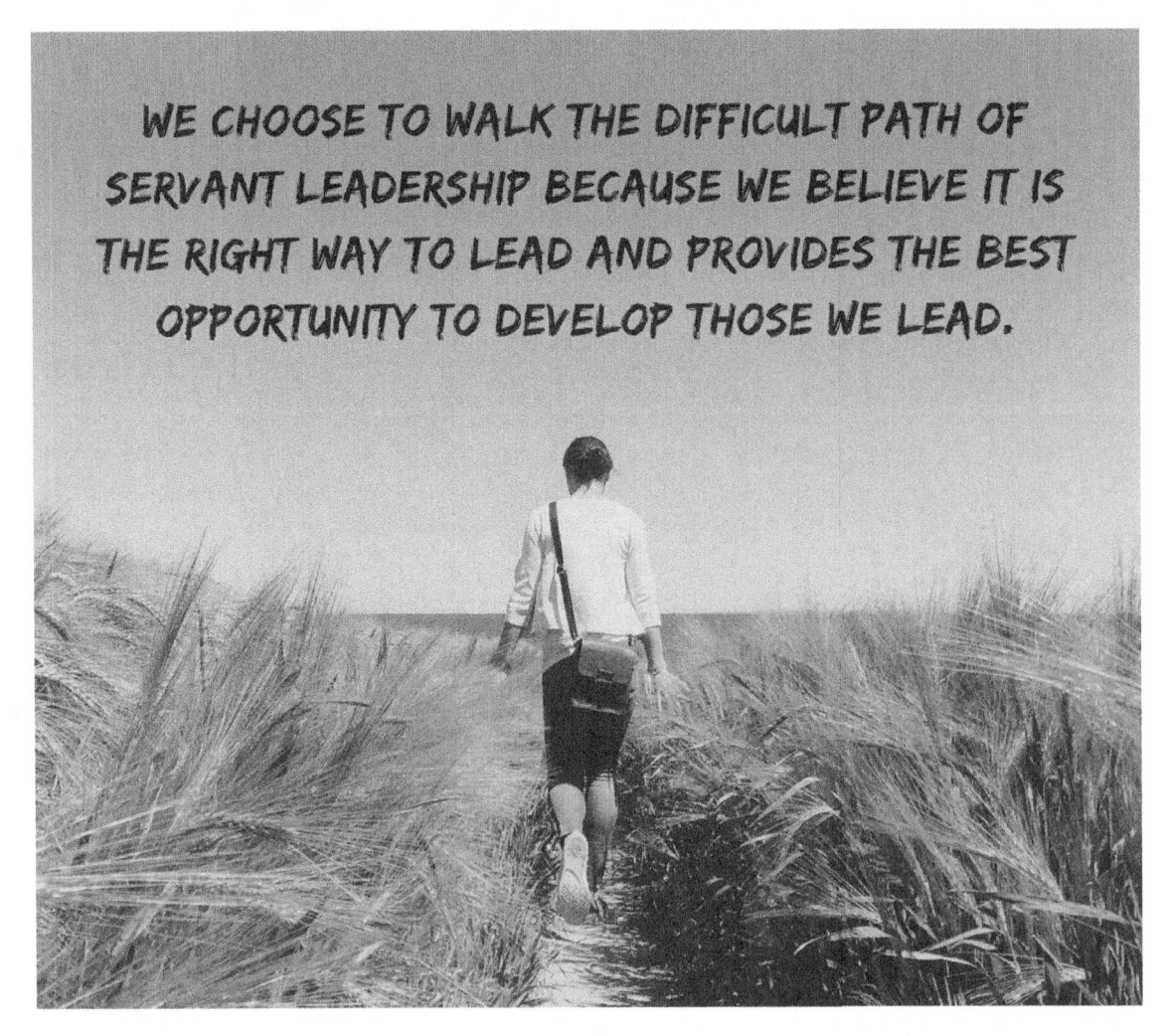

> WE CHOOSE TO WALK THE DIFFICULT PATH OF SERVANT LEADERSHIP BECAUSE WE BELIEVE IT IS THE RIGHT WAY TO LEAD AND PROVIDES THE BEST OPPORTUNITY TO DEVELOP THOSE WE LEAD.

Day 39

Thinking like a Leader

Develop a Mindset of Servant Leadership

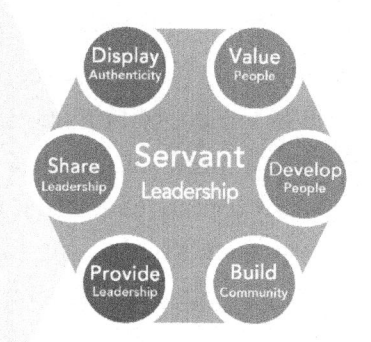

"Everybody can be great because anybody can serve. You don't have to have a college degree to serve. You don't have to make your subject and verb agree to serve. You only need a heart full of grace. A soul generated by love."
– Martin Luther King, Jr.

Is it natural to want to serve others? A study conducted by Felix Warneken and Michael Tomasello at the Max Planck Institute demonstrated that children as young as 18 months will help an adult in need. They concluded that "even very young children have a *natural* tendency to help other persons solve their problems, even when the other is a stranger and they receive no benefit at all." So, is it possible that serving others is more natural than we think and that our tendency toward self-interest builds in us over the years?

Robert Greenleaf spoke of the "natural" desire that people have to serve others. "The servant-leader is servant first . . . It begins with the natural feeling that one wants to serve, to serve first. Then conscious choice brings one to aspire to lead. That person is sharply different from one who is leader first; perhaps because of the need to assuage an unusual power drive or to acquire material possessions . . .The leader-first and the servant-first are two extreme types. Between them there are shadings and blends that are part of the infinite variety of human nature." Our journey in this workbook has been to take us back to a more natural state when it felt right to serve others, when we were servant-first rather than leader-first people. This servant mindset is what we are after. We want to go beyond acting like a servant to actually thinking like a servant. We want to see our role as leaders be primarily to serve for the good of those we lead.

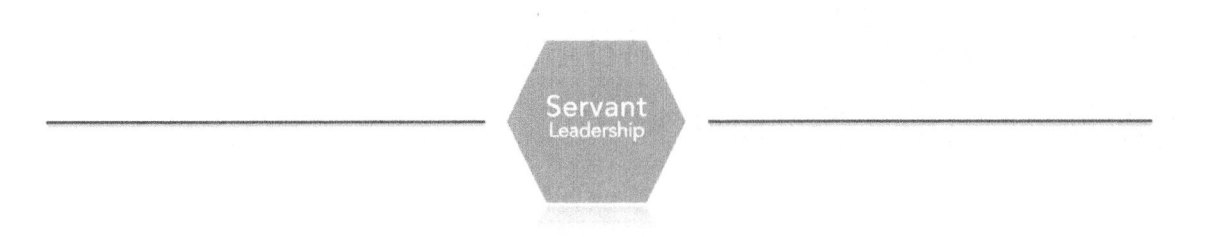

Personal Reflection

- What is the difference between being servant-first vs. leader-first? Which of these most characterizes my leadership?

- How do I manage my natural desires to serve with the constant pull toward self-interest?

- To whom am I accountable? Who is my mentor in developing myself as a servant leader?

Group Reflection

- How can we create positive accountability for displaying servant leadership attitudes and actions?

- Do we think serving is *natural?* Do people really want to help others, or is our more natural tendency to take care of ourselves first?

Practice – Action steps

- Make a short list of servant-first actions and act on one of those today.

- Establish 3 goals for increasing your servant leadership over the next 3 months.

Day 40

Acting like a Leader

Increase the Competencies of Servant Leadership

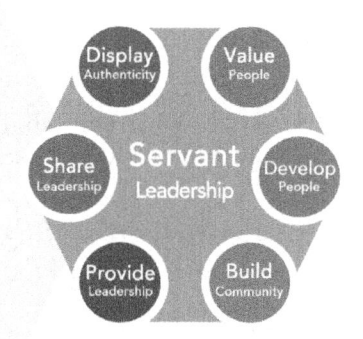

When he was just nineteen years old, Kent Keith penned the Paradoxical Commandments which have been shared around the world as an encouragement for leaders who sometimes find the leadership journey to be just too difficult. Kent had the opportunity to visit Mother Teresa's program in Calcutta, India and saw on the wall a copy of the Paradoxical Commandments he had written many years before. We never know where one of our leadership actions will go and how many people these actions will influence. As you face leadership challenges today, consider the deep wisdom of these "commandments."

The Paradoxical Commandments

1. People are illogical, unreasonable, and self-centered. Love them anyway.
2. If you do good, people will accuse you of selfish ulterior motives. Do good anyway.
3. If you are successful, you will win false friends and true enemies. Succeed anyway.
4. The good you do today will be forgotten tomorrow. Do good anyway.
5. Honesty and frankness make you vulnerable. Be honest and frank anyway.
6. The biggest men and women with the biggest ideas can be shot down by the smallest men and women with the smallest minds. Think big anyway.
7. People favor underdogs but follow only top dogs. Fight for a few underdogs anyway.
8. What you spend years building may be destroyed overnight. Build anyway.
9. People really need help but may attack you if you do help them. Help people anyway.

10. Give the world the best you have and you'll get kicked in the teeth. Give the best you have anyway.

If I can dare to add one more to this list . . .

11. People may see your servant leadership efforts as signs of weakness and may misunderstand the unique power in how you lead. Lead as a servant anyway.

Yes, lead according to your beliefs, stay true to your values, live each day as if you believe that the best way to lead others, the best way to enhance your organization, the best way to make a difference in the world is to become an effective servant leader.

Personal Reflection

- Do I consider myself more of a servant leader now than when I began this workbook? Why?

- How do I describe the kind of leader I desire to become?

- Am I committed to pursuing this goal of becoming a servant-first leader?

Group Reflection

- Is our leadership team committed to servant leadership practice?

- Is our organization a servant-minded organization?

- What can we do to improve?

Practice – Action steps

- Read more about servant leadership,

- Practice servant leadership behaviors (Display Authenticity, Value People, Develop People, Build Community, Provide Leadership, and Share Leadership).

- Assess your own leadership practice and that of your organization.

Conclusion
Final Thoughts

At the beginning of this workbook, I invited you to join me on a journey of servant leadership learning and change. I hope that this journey has been one of meaningful discovery and growth. Servant leadership requires a life-long commitment to putting others first and leading according to your deepest beliefs and values. My hope is that this workbook has taken you down paths that show the difficulty but also the possibilities inherent in this challenging approach to leadership. Servant leadership is not the easy path. It is much easier to use our power and authority to get things done. We will appear strong and effective if we do. But, we know that there is a better way. A better way to motivate people to not just follow, but to lead themselves and to build an organization that puts it's people first and through this clear focus, accomplishes much more than they ever thought possible.

Are you a servant leader? Is your organization servant-minded? The only way to effectively answer that question is to ask your people to provide honest and candid feedback. This can be done through simply asking them or by conducting focus groups, or by formal assessment (like with the OLA assessment tools provided through Servant Leader Performance). I want to encourage you to make organizational assessment a regular part of your organizations strategic growth and development plan. We need to know what our people are actually experiencing and we need to find safe ways for them to tell us.

I wish you all the best as you continue this journey. If this workbook has been useful to you, share it with someone else. Encourage others to consider this approach to leading to engage their minds, hearts and spirits to create organizations that are authentic, that value and develop people, that build community and that provide and share leadership. We can build better, stronger and healthier organizations and it begins with a commitment to serve those that we lead. God bless. --- *Jim Laub*

James Laub Ed.D.

Additional tools
from Servant Leader Performance

Servant Leader Performance is an organization committed to help you and your organization become healthier and more servant-minded. Consider using assessment tools that will help you better understand how you are viewed as a leader by those you lead or how everyone in your organization views the health of your organization and its leadership.

The **Organizational Leadership Assessment** (OLA) – the OLA is a web-delivered instrument that provides assessment of your organization's health from a values-based, servant leadership perspective. The instrument is designed to be taken by people at all position levels (Top Leaders, Supervisors/Managers & Workforce). The report provides an organizational health level, perception match between the three position levels and your organization's readiness for change. The instrument takes only 15 minutes to complete and sub-group reports can be provided along with your overall organizational analysis.

The **Servant Leader Performance (SLP) Assessment** – the SLP is a web-based review that provides anonymous, multi-angle performance assessment of individual leaders. Individual leaders can be assessed from the perspective of self, supervisor, coworkers and direct reports. These reviews provide concrete, result-based feedback and encourage open interaction and communication driving strategies for personal and professional improvement.

www.ServantLeaderPerformance.com

Author
James Laub, Ed.D.

Dr. James Laub serves as Professor of Leadership at the MacArthur School of Leadership at Palm Beach Atlantic University and oversees the Master's in Leadership program.

He is the president of Servant Leader Performance and the creator of the Organizational Leadership Assessment (OLA) which measures organizational health from a servant leadership perspective and of the SLP assessment which is used for assessing individual leadership performance.

Jim received his doctorate in Educational Leadership: Adult Education from Florida Atlantic University. His dissertation and ongoing research has focused on the critical topic of servant leadership and organizational health. He is a facilitator, a trainer, a speaker and a tool-maker for organizational effectiveness.

Contact Jim Laub at Servant Leader Performance:

Jim Laub, Ed.D.
Servant Leader Performance
18240 Lake Bend Drive
Jupiter, FL, 33458

www.ServantLeaderPerformance.com
jlaub@servantleaderperformance.com

Made in the USA
Coppell, TX
01 March 2021